HAND LETTERING

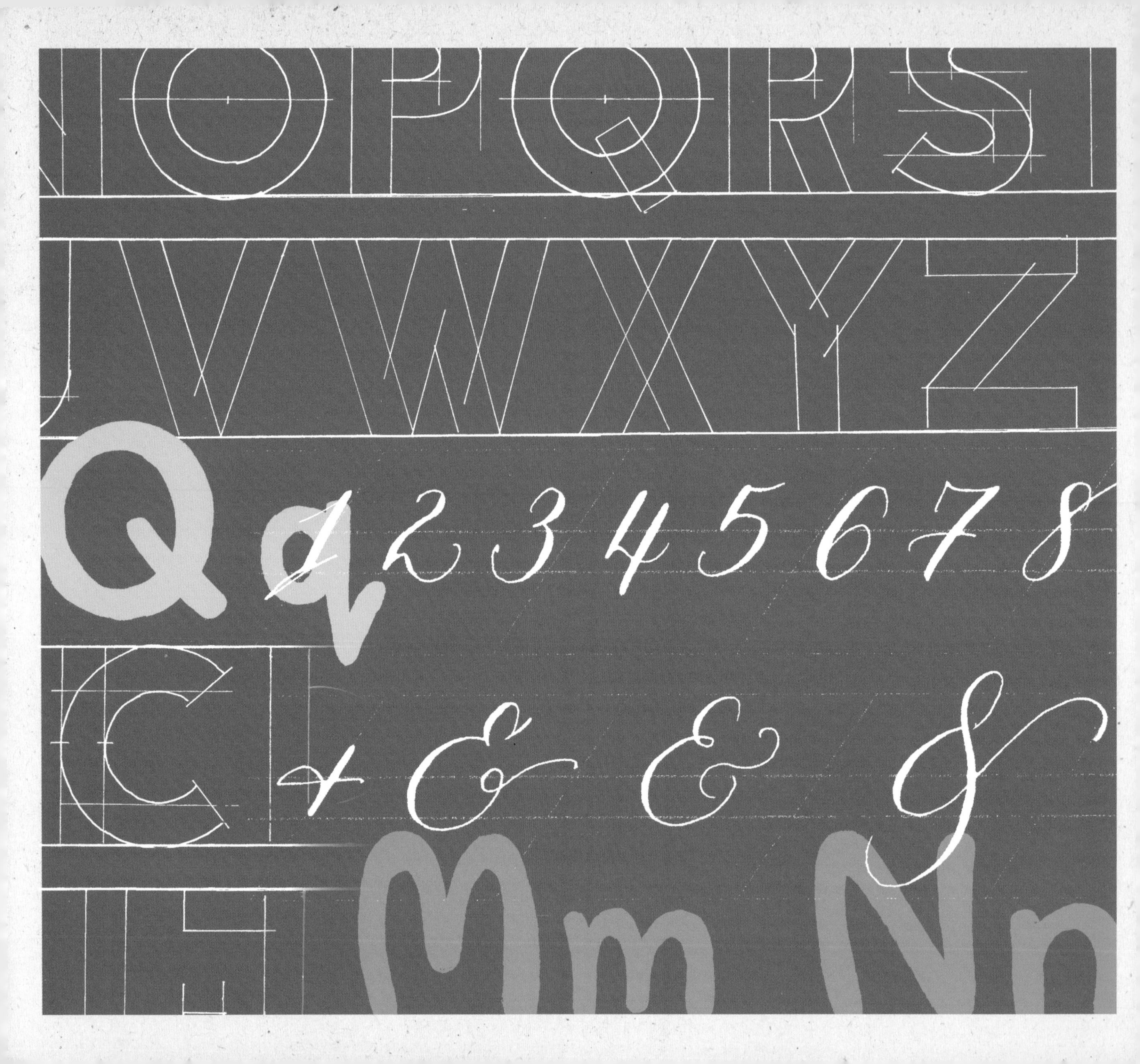
OPQRS
VWXYZ
Qq
12345678
& & &
Mm Nn

HAND LETTERING

A beginner's guide to modern calligraphy, brushwork scripts, and blackboard letter art

Judy Broad, Archie Salandin, and Michael Tilley

This edition published in 2018 by Arcturus Publishing Limited
26/27 Bickels Yard, 151–153 Bermondsey Street,
London SE1 3HA

ISBN: 978-1-78828-623-7
AD006051UK

Printed in China

Contents

Introduction

Hand lettering is all around us—from wedding stationery, shop signs, pub menus and house numbers to movie posters, music album covers, commercial packaging and urban clothing. Once you start looking for it, you'll notice it everywhere, and you'll see that it comes in a vast array of typographic styles.

Historically, hand lettering in the West began with the Latin alphabet in Rome around 600 BC. Originally, letters were carved into stone, and later they were painted onto walls and on the pages of religious texts. The skills needed to produce hand-written lettering developed and were refined over time, largely due to the practice of copying the Bible. By medieval times, lettering had become ornate and colourful, the first letter of each chapter of a book often being beautifully illuminated.

The invention of the printing press in the 15th century brought about a huge decline in hand-written manuscripts, however, the art did not die out completely. In more recent times, designers such as Eric Gill—who created the typeface still used today on the London Underground—revived the art of hand lettering and safeguarded its popularity into the 20th and 21st centuries.

If you'd like to try creating your own unique and decorative hand lettering, this practical book is an excellent place to start. It is aimed at the absolute beginner and will guide you through all the fundamentals.

The book is divided into sections covering three distinct hand-lettering crafts: modern calligraphy, brush lettering and blackboard letter art. Each of these sections is presented by an expert artist, introducing you to their craft and providing a range of different typographic styles for you to discover and practise.

Whether you'd like to make a home-made birthday card, a decoration for your home, some eye-catching text for your website or business, or if you're even thinking about going into the professional signwriting business, the pages that follow will inspire you to get a nib, brush or paint pen and get started on a highly rewarding journey.

THE ARTIST IS NOT A DIFFERENT KIND OF PERSON, BUT EVERY PERSON IS A DIFFERENT KIND OF ARTIST

ERIC GILL

COFFEE
WHISKEY

Jean Jacques & Amelie
116 RUE DE LA VALENTINE
MARSEILLES 84300
Eric & Ellinor
HAGAGATAN 16
SE-118 89 STOCKHOLM
thank you
Surprise
love

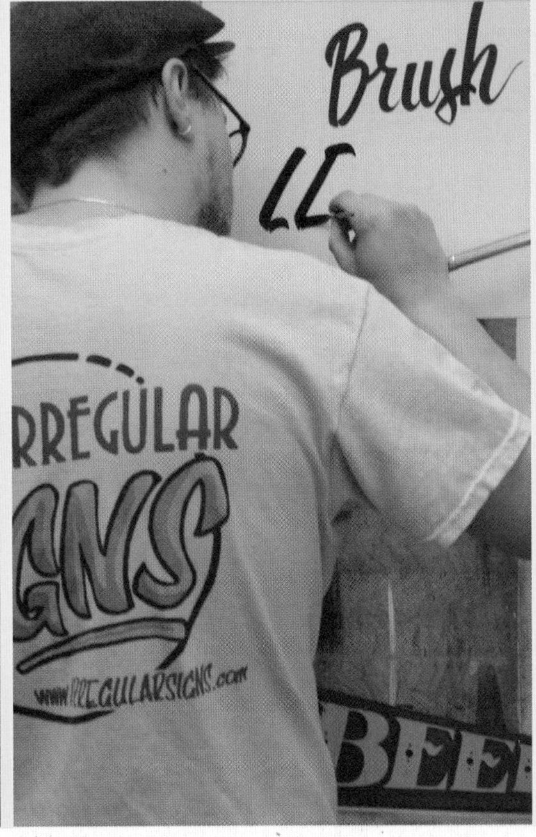
Brush

LIVE
DJ
COCKTAILS FOR £15
COCKTAIL TEAPOTS £15

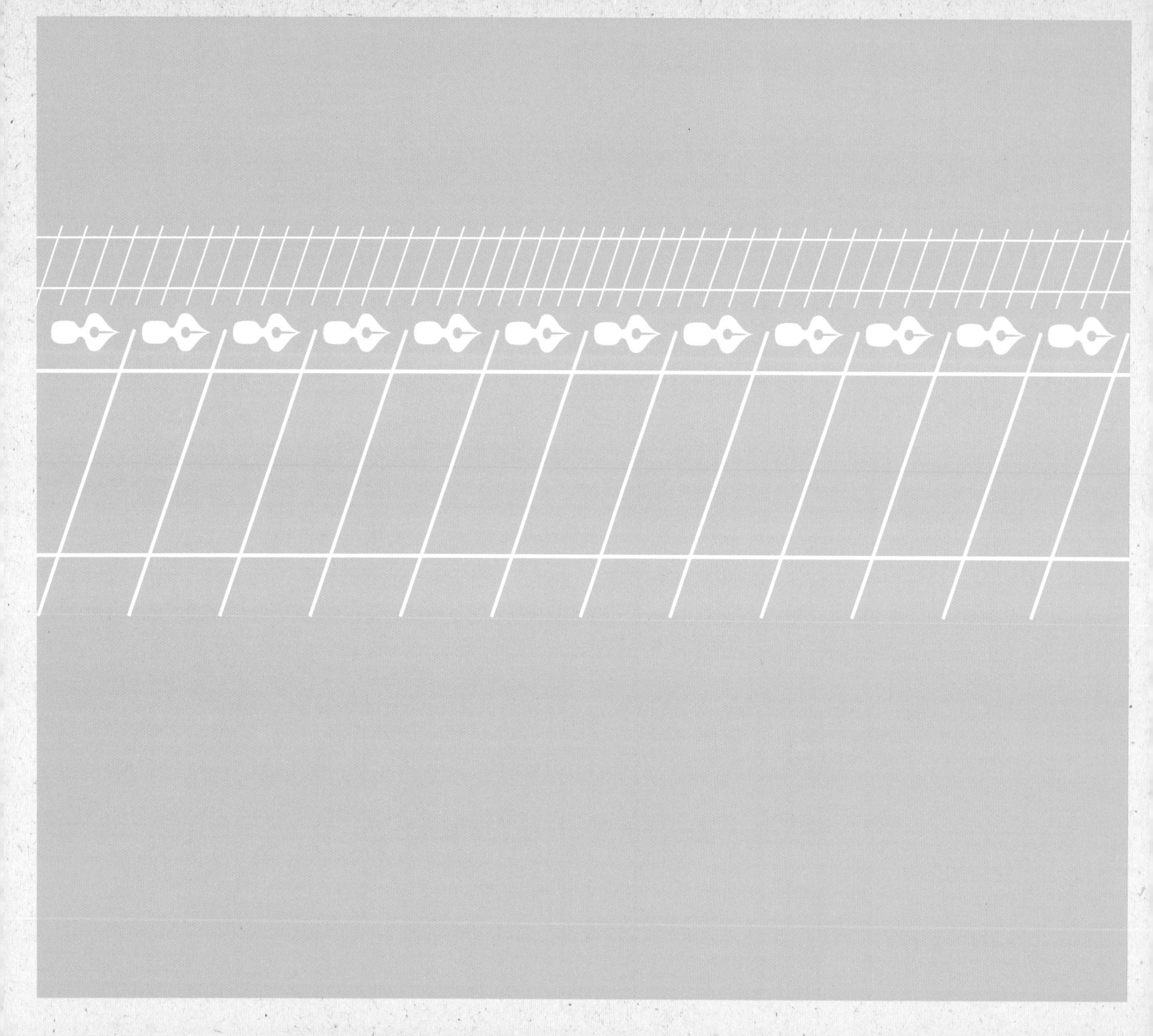

MODERN
CALLIGRAPHY

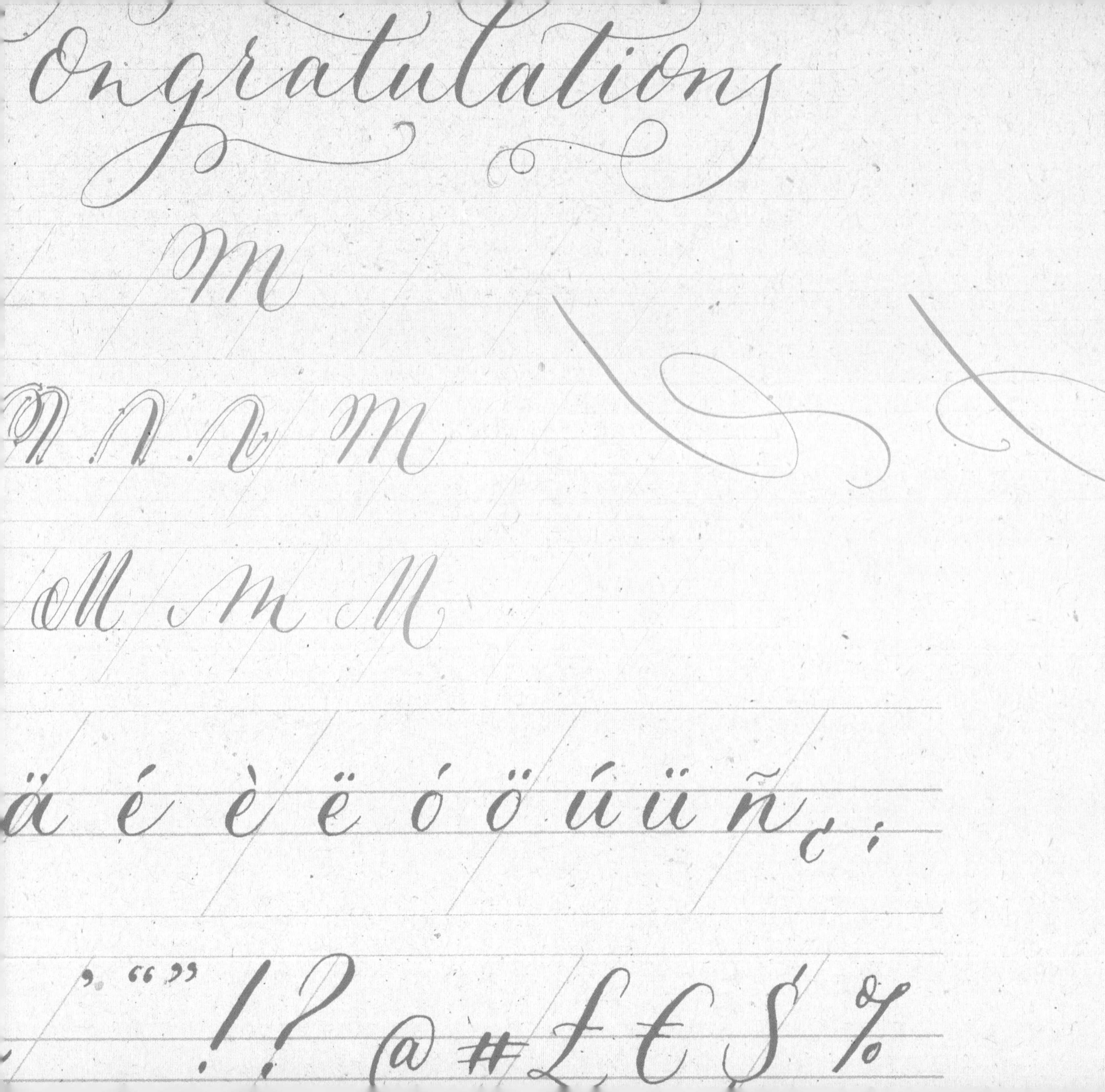
ongratulations
M
M
M M
ä é è ë ó ö ú ü ñ ¿ ¡
, " " ! ? @ # £ € $ %

Contents

About the artist

I was first introduced to calligraphy by an art teacher whilst still at school and became instantly hooked. My trusty penholder and little tin of nibs accompanied me wherever I went and I volunteered my services to anyone who showed any interest. Then life got busy and I forgot about calligraphy for a while.

My passion was reignited about five years ago when my niece was getting married. She asked me if I could still do 'the fancy writing' and I went in search of my penholders and little tin of nibs. I discovered that I could indeed still do the 'fancy writing' and fell back in love with calligraphy. I then enrolled on various courses and workshops and dedicated my free time to improving my calligraphy skills.

Today I work as a professional calligrapher from my studio in Surrey in the UK, and have been lucky enough to work on a whole host of exciting projects. I have worked with many brides, helping to add that personal and unique touch to their wedding stationery as well as working with prestigious corporate clients such as Chanel, Aspinal of London, Waitrose, Christian Dior and Ferrero Rocher. My work has been featured in many blogs and publications associated with the wedding industry. As well as commission work, I enjoy passing on my calligraphy skills through my workshop programme throughout the UK and abroad.

Calligraphy has been defined as 'the art of beautiful penmanship'. In our digital age, it is a pleasure and refreshing to receive something beautifully hand written. I believe that calligraphy undoubtedly adds something personal and unique to your event or occasion.

Judy Broad
www.judybroadcalligraphy.co.uk

About modern calligraphy

There are many things I love about calligraphy: I love the rhythm of the pen, I love the sound of the nib gliding across the paper, I love watching the glossy ink drying on the page, and I love seeing people's reactions when they receive something beautifully hand written. Now I cannot imagine life without calligraphy; I have found it rewarding and relaxing. When I embark on a calligraphy project, I become totally immersed in what I am doing and time just flies by.

The following pages will focus on a modern calligraphy style. While the foundation of modern calligraphy comes from a more traditional script, modern calligraphy is a more relaxed and style. Experiment, be creative and you will develop your own lettering style.

After being shown the basic materials and techniques, you will be guided through how to build a good foundation for letterforms and taught how to perfect them. Although this style is a modern variation, there is a definite nod to traditional pointed pen calligraphy because, as Pablo Picasso said, you should 'Learn the rules like a pro, so you can break them like an artist.'

If you make time for practice, your efforts will be rewarded. Experiment and take inspiration from all around you and above all have fun on your very own calligraphy journey. In this digital age, it is refreshing to come away from our computer screens and mobile phones and be creative. You should remember to feel inspired by what you can create.

So give it a try and get ready to watch the magic happen!

LEARN THE RULES LIKE A PRO, SO YOU CAN BREAK THEM LIKE AN ARTIST

PABLO PICASSO

Brett & Sandra Winter
2196 Washington St
Madison, WI
48253
Victoria & Will Lott
63 Herband Street
Cuba

Supplies and materials

YOUR ESSENTIAL CALLIGRAPHY TOOLKIT

Before you can get started, you are going to need the right calligraphy tools.

One of the great things about calligraphy is that you don't actually need very much to get started. To begin with, you will need a pen holder, nib, ink and some paper.

We will take a look at each of these to enable you to have the confidence to make some informed choices and get started on your calligraphy journey. I would encourage you to purchase quality supplies. Fortunately, most calligraphy supplies are not too expensive, and you will find that using quality ones will really make a difference to your finished work.

If you are left-handed, please read the information on page 69 before buying a pen holder.

PEN HOLDERS

There are a multitude of pen holders to choose from, which can be confusing for a complete beginner. The first choice you will need to make is whether to use an oblique or a straight pen holder.

The oblique pen holder was introduced to help people learning copperplate styles of script. Copperplate is written on a slant of 55 degrees. An oblique pen holder has an extra part attached to the side, known as the flange, which holds the nib. By using this type of pen holder, the nib is positioned at the correct offset angle, and this in turn will help you to make an even, smooth-edged down stroke.

Straight pen holders, on the other hand, are just that—straight. They may vary in width, length, colour and shape. Some may be curved to fit more comfortably in the hand, and some have some cork cushioning which can make them more comfortable to use for a long period of time.

For the lettering style in this part of the book you can use an oblique or a straight pen holder—it really comes down to personal preference.

As the majority of pen holders are relatively inexpensive, my advice would be to try a few and see what works best for you.

Tip

If you use a slanted lettering style, you may prefer an oblique pen holder. If, on the other hand, you prefer a more upright style, you could try a straight one.

NIBS

Your next decision is which nib to use. This can be a little daunting when you are faced with so many different types and brands.

For the lettering styles in this part of the book, you want a nib that is designed for pointed pen calligraphy. These nibs have a sharp pointed tip as opposed to a broad or flat edge (used for italic and other calligraphy scripts).

Pointed pen nibs do vary in size, shape and flexibility. With a more flexible nib, the tines at the point separate more readily, which will give a greater swell to your strokes. A more flexible nib will require more control, so it may be best to start with a nib with more of a medium flex such as Nikko G. The name of the nib is usually etched onto the body of the nib.

As with pen holders, my advice is to try a few and find out what works best for you and the particular project that you are working on.

Guide to nibs

Nikko G: This hand-cut nib from Japan is a popular choice for both beginners and experienced calligraphers. It has a medium flex, is long lasting and produces a smooth stroke.

Zebra G: Also made in Japan, this nib is similar to the Nikko G. It is a little sharper and more flexible, and will give a finer hairline.

Gillot 404: This is a good nib for beginners, and will give you a fine hairline.

Gillot 303: This is a little more flexible than the 404, and therefore a little harder to control. It is a sharply pointed nib that produces good swells and elegant hairlines.

Hunt 56: This is similar to the Gillot 404 in terms of flexibility, and is a good choice for beginners.

Hunt 101: This is a reliable and long-lasting nib. For slightly larger lettering, this is a good choice.

Brause 66F: This is a very flexible nib and can therefore be a bit tricky for a beginner. It will produce thick down strokes and fine hairlines, and can be useful when creating larger lettering.

Preparing a nib

Brand new nibs require 'prepping' before you use them for the first time.

Although not normally visible, most new nibs will have a protective lacquer designed to protect them during transport and while in storage. You need to remove this protective layer, and this can be done in one of the following ways:

- Wash in mild washing-up liquid, then rinse in warm water and dry.

- Wipe your nib with some toothpaste straight from the tube. Then wash off and dry.

- Run your nib backwards and forwards through a naked flame for a couple of seconds.

If the nib is not prepared properly, you will find your ink tends to pool and stick onto the nib, and ink flow will be hindered.

Caring for your nibs

As you work, it is advisable to wash your nib regularly to prevent too much build-up of ink and to ensure even ink flow. Just swish it around in a small jar of water and dry it before you continue. When you have finished what you are working on, make sure you remove the nib from its pen holder, then clean and dry it well. You can use a soft toothbrush to clean your nib, and then store it away safely in a small tin or jar until you need it again.

How long will a nib last?

I am often asked this question, and it is a tricky one to answer as there really isn't a steadfast rule with pointed pen nibs. If the tines become separated or bent, it is time for a new nib. Equally, if your nib isn't working as well for you—it might be scratchy or your may have lost a crisp hairline—it is probably time for a new one. As a rough guide, when I am addressing envelopes I tend to change my nib every 40 to 50 envelopes.

Calli ink

Sumi ink

Higgins Eternal ink

INK

I recommend starting with black bottled ink while you master the basics. Later you can try gouache, watercolour, or even grind your own ink from a Sumi stick.

Bottled ink is probably the easiest option for beginners, as it is generally the right consistency to use straight from the bottle.

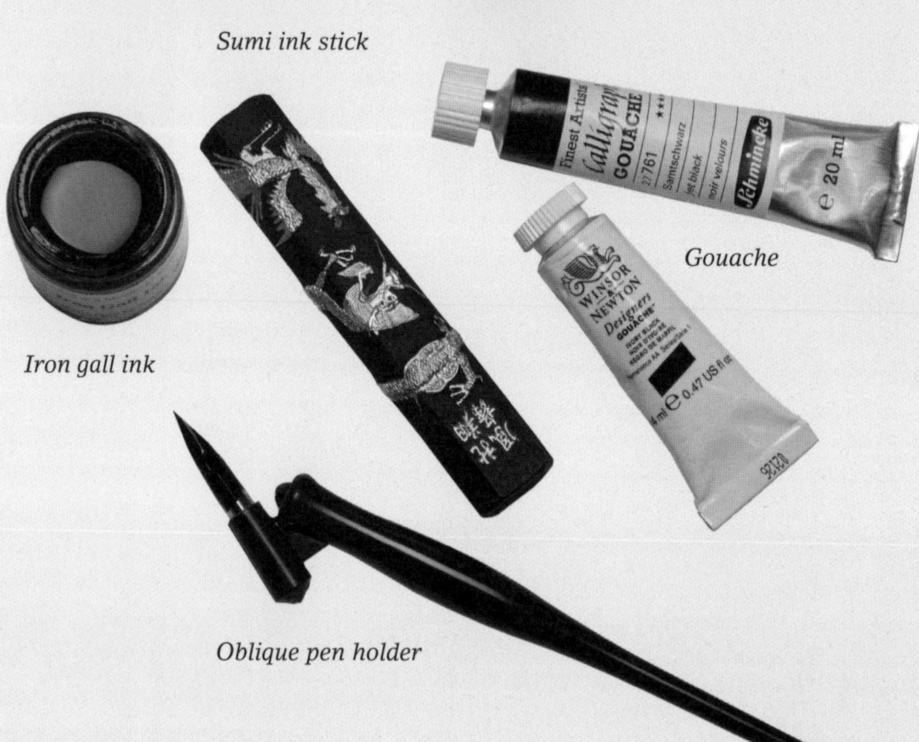

Sumi ink stick

Gouache

Iron gall ink

Oblique pen holder

Black

I would suggest a bottle of quality permanent black ink, which will not fade over time. It is best to stay away from fountain-pen inks. They tend to be a thinner consistency which can cause the ink to bleed on the paper, and they don't produce a dense black colour.

My favourite black inks include Higgins Eternal, which flows nicely from the nib, and Japanese Sumi inks made from oil soot, which have a nice glossy finish when dry.

Gold

When it comes to choosing gold and other metallic inks for your hand lettering, I have a few firm favourites that are worth trying.

Dr. Ph. Martin's Copper Plate Gold is an acrylic ink that produces a beautiful iridescent sparkle on your page. You can use it straight from the bottle, but using this ink can be a little tricky so there are a couple of things worth knowing.

First of all, before you use the ink you will need to give the bottle a vigorous shake so the gold pigment is evenly dispersed. This can sometimes take a few minutes. As you work on a project, you will need to stop every so often to shake it again to keep the gold pigment evenly dispersed.

Secondly, because it is an acrylic ink, it can be tough to clean from your nib if it is left to dry. As you finish writing or even if you are just having a break, make sure you wash and clean your nib thoroughly.

Also worth trying is the Finetec Gold palette, which has five different shades of gold and a silver. You use them in the same way as you would a watercolour block or pan, and they too can give a stunning effect.

White

There are a number of different white inks or paints available, but Dr. Ph. Martin's Bleedproof White is undoubtedly my favourite. This is essentially a correction fluid, but when mixed with some water to the right consistency, it flows well through the nib and is wonderfully opaque on coloured paper.

Other whites that are popular in calligraphy are:

- Moon Palace White Sumi
- Dr. Ph. Martin's Pen White
- Ziller North Wind White
- Winsor & Newton White Calligraphy Ink

So there you have some of my favourite calligraphy inks and colours that I use on a daily basis, but it is by no means an exhaustive list. As always, my advice is to experiment and discover what works best for you.

PAPER

As a general rule, smooth, uncoated papers work best with a dip pen and ink. However, it is worth noting that not all things are equal in the world of paper. Some papers may work with the nib and ink you are using, but others may be problematic. It can sometimes be tricky to use textured and rough papers because the tines of your nib can easily catch in the paper fibers, causing the ink to splatter.

It really is a question of trial and error to discover what works well for you. I enjoy different coloured papers and envelopes, which can really add some personality to calligraphy projects.

For practice, I typically prefer to use either Rhodia pads or a premium printer paper. Rhodia pads are a favourite among calligraphers for their super-smooth qualities, and they are thin enough to pop a guide sheet underneath, which is ideal for perfecting your letters. A good-quality printer paper can give good results; the cheaper ones may cause the ink to bleed.

I also like to have a supply of Bristol board, which is lovely and smooth, and some watercolour paper.

USEFUL ADDITIONS

You may find some of the following items useful to have to hand:

Mechanical pencil: You will be reaching for a pencil for sketching out layouts, drawing guidelines and even practising your letterforms. Most calligraphers favour a mechanical pencil (0.3 or 0.5 mm) for a fine, sharp line. If you want to work on dark papers, a chalk pencil is also invaluable.

Rubber/eraser: The white plastic erasers that are widely available are perfect for erasing pencil lines, and click erasers can also be useful when extra care and precision is needed.

Ruler: You will find an acrylic or metal ruler indispensible. I favour the transparent acrylic ones to aid with the ruling of lines, and if they have a stainless-steel cutting edge, even better!

Getting started

BASIC SET-UP

It is important to be mindful of how you sit to avoid any aches and pains in your neck, shoulders and back. Try to sit square to the table you are working on, with your shoulders straight and both feet planted on the floor. Aim for a straight back and avoid being hunched over your work. It is worth checking your posture every so often.

If you are right-handed, have your ink, a small jar of water, a lint-free cloth and a small scrap piece of paper (often referred to as a scratch sheet) to your right. If you are left-handed, you will want everything safely on your left. It is also helpful to have a few sheets of paper under the sheet you are working on, to provide a bit of cushioning.

Insert your nib into your oblique or straight holder. When I am teaching workshops, I suggest laying the pen holder vertically on the page with the flange (the extra bit) to the left, and insert the nib so it's pointing in the direction of your slant line and so it is sitting flat over the page (as shown in the photograph). If you are using a straight pen holder, you just need to slot the nib into the end of the pen holder. There may be a rim or prongs to hold it. The nib needs to feel secure when you write, so if it feels a bit wobbly, it may need pushing in a bit further.

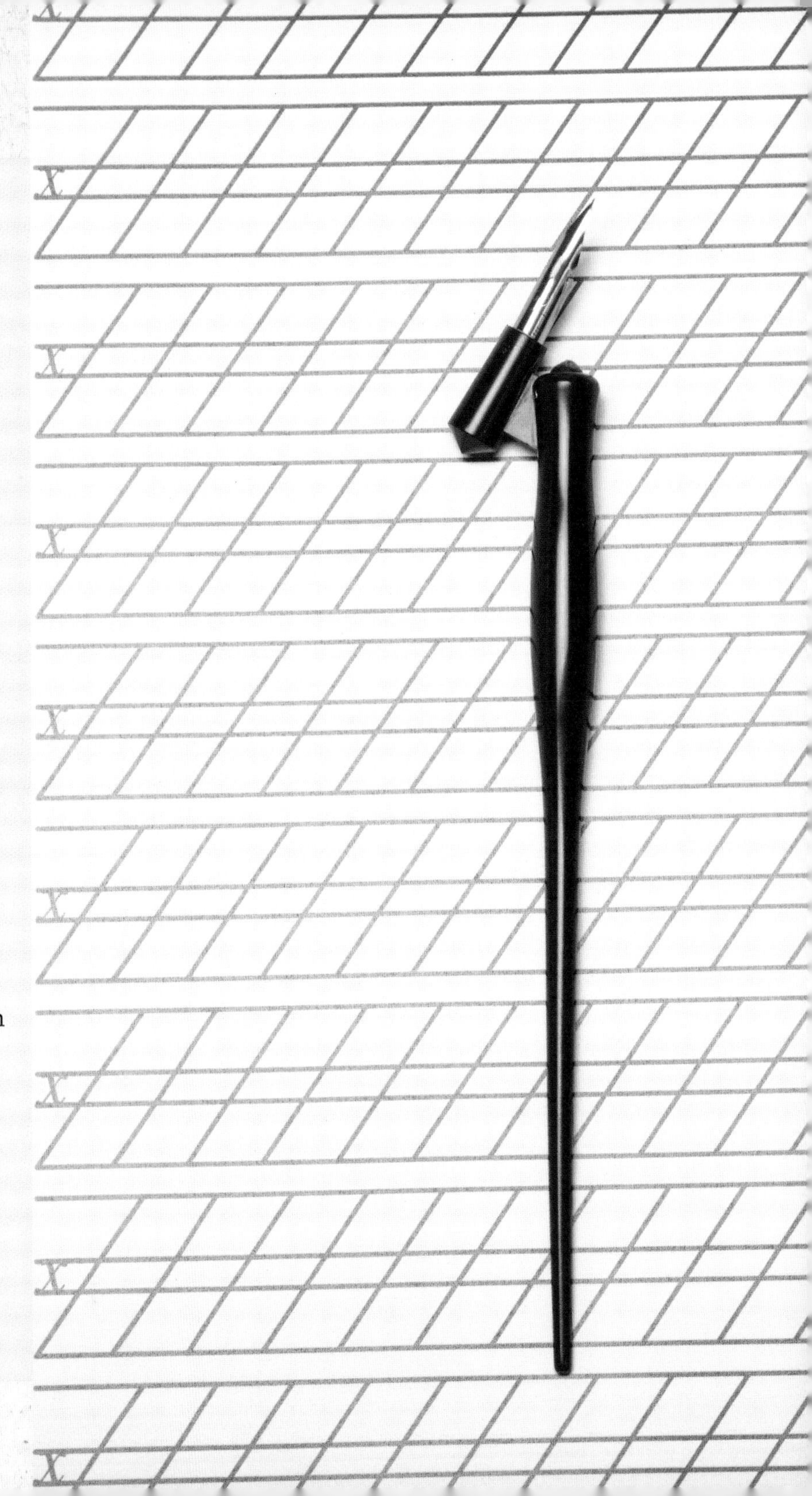

HOW TO HOLD A PEN

Aim to keep a light grip, and try to keep your hand and arm as relaxed as possible.

Hold the pen fairly low down to give you stability, and let the pen holder rest in the space between your thumb and index finger. The pen holder should be slanting backwards rather than standing upright. If the pen is too upright you may find your nib catches on the paper, causing the ink to splatter.

If you are left-handed, you may find a straight pen holder better to work with (see information on page 69).

HOW TO DIP

When you are ready to begin, dip your nib into the ink so the ink covers the small hole on the top of the nib. This hole (known as a vent) acts as a reservoir and will help your ink to flow smoothly and evenly. If you feel you have too much ink on the nib, wipe any excess on the rim of the bottle. I then test the flow on my scratch sheet. Remember, you need to have prepared the nib before using it for the first time (see page 19).

THE PRESSURE AND RELEASE RULE

We are nearly ready to begin, but before we do, it is important to be aware of the pressure and release rule.

Every time you make a downward stroke, apply some pressure. When you apply pressure the tines on the nib will open, allowing more ink to be released, and you will achieve a thicker stroke.

When you make an upward stroke you will release the pressure. When you release the pressure the tines on the nib will close, and you will make a thinner, hairline stroke.

This has become known as 'the pressure and release rule', and will give your letterforms thick and thin strokes. It is this contrast that I really love in pointed pen calligraphy, and this is what will make your letters stand out. Guidelines or grid lines will help you to become familiar with the slant of your letters, and also their size and proportions.

The diagram below shows one section of a typical grid line sheet. It contains a series of horizontal and diagonal lines. You could make your own template of a gridline sheet to use as a guide, or you can download an A4 (US letter size) guideline sheet from my website: www.judybroadcalligraphy.co.uk.

You can either write directly onto the grid line sheets, or you can position the gridline under the paper that you are writing on.

Base line: letters will traditionally sit on the base line. This is the line you write on.
Waist line: the line directly above the base line. This marks the top of lower case letters such as 'o', 'a', 'c', and so on.
Ascender line: lower case letters with ascenders (e.g. 'b', 'l', 'h') will extend up to this line.
Descender line: lower case letters with descenders (e.g. 'g', 'j', 'y') will extend down to this line.

Lower case letters without descender or ascender loops will fit between the base line and the waist line. Upper case letters will fit in the space from the base line to the ascender line.

Slant lines: These are drawn at an angle of 55 degrees, which was the angle originally used for traditional copperplate calligraphy. The lettering style used in this part of the book is loosely based on a copperplate hand, but with a contemporary feel and look. All of your down strokes should follow this slant line. It is, however, perfectly fine to adopt a more upright style—the principal aim is to be consistent in your letterforms.

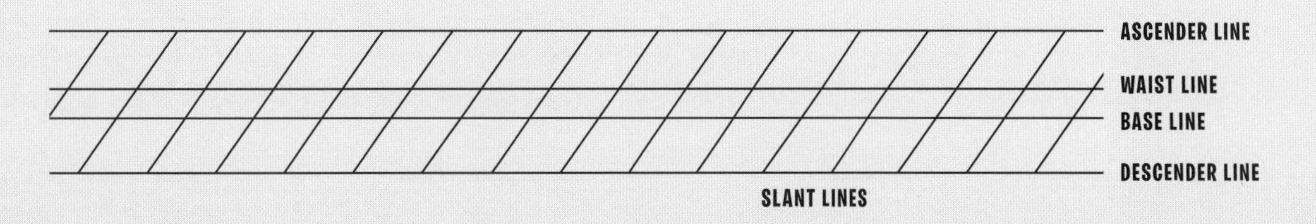

Putting pen to paper

BASIC STROKES

It is worthwhile dedicating some time to perfecting your basic strokes. By doing so, you will become confident using a dip pen and a pointed pen nib, and you will be learning the strokes that will be used to form your letters. Practising these strokes will also build muscle memory, making the process quicker in the long run.

Before you start, here are a few tips and reminders of what you need to be conscious of:

- When you make a downward stroke, you apply pressure to achieve a thicker stroke.
- When you make an upward stroke, you release the pressure to achieve a fine hairline.
- The tip of the nib should point in the direction of your slant line.
- Aim to use the whole of the tip of the nib. If your nib is rotated, you will not achieve a stroke with even pressure.
- If you are right-handed, it can sometimes help to slightly rotate your page to the left. If you are left-handed, it can help to rotate it to the right. Ultimately, find whatever works best for you.
- Keep your hand and arm relaxed.
- Proceed at a fairly slow and steady pace. Calligraphy is an art. Imagine you are drawing each stroke and letter rather than writing at your usual speed.
- Lastly, relax, breathe and enjoy the journey!

Take each of the basic strokes on the pages that follow one at a time. Look where the stroke starts and ends, which direction your hand should move in, and where the pressure is applied. Complete a line or two before moving onto the next one. When you have completed one stroke form, take a minute to reflect on which of your strokes worked well or where you could improve.

Downward stroke

◀ Aim for even pressure from the start to the end of the stroke. You can achieve a squared-off top and bottom by pausing at the beginning and the end of the stroke.

Hairline stroke

◀ This is an upward stroke with no pressure. It should curve slightly upwards, and is used as an entry and exit stroke. The pen should just lightly glide up the page.

Pressure and release stroke

◀ Start with a downward stroke with pressure. Release the pressure just before you come to the base line, and then curve to the right and come up with no pressure, creating a hairline. Your upstroke should be parallel to your downward stroke.

Oval

◀ Here, we are looking for an oval shape as opposed to a rounded one. Start towards the top with no pressure and move in an anti-clockwise direction. As you curve over to the left-hand side, gradually apply your pressure. Release the pressure before you come to the base line, and curve up with a hairline to complete the oval.

Ascender stroke

◀ Start with a hairline stroke that curves upwards to the right. As you reach the ascender line, curve over to the left before coming down with pressure. To achieve the squared-off end to the stroke, don't forget to pause as you complete the stroke. Pay attention to the shape of your loop too. You don't want it too fat or too skinny.

Descender stroke

◀ Aim for even pressure as you form a downward stroke, and gradually release the pressure before you curve upwards with a hairline, creating your loop. As with the ascender stroke, pay attention to the shape of the loop—not too fat or too skinny.

Capital stem

◀ It is very important to master this 'swelled' stroke. It begins with a slight curve and no pressure. As you travel downwards, apply the pressure in the middle of the stroke. Then start to release the pressure and finish with a slight upward curve. Your curves at the start and finish of the stroke need to be gentle and should not have sharp hooks. Imagine following the shape of a ladle and you will have a beautiful capital stem.

Loop

◀ Begin with a hairline stroke curving upwards. Once you reach the ascender line, curve over to the right and apply pressure as you travel down in a clockwise direction. Release your pressure and curve up again, creating an oval loop. Cross the downward stroke just under the ascender line.

Letters and characters

This section guides you through the letters of the alphabet and is where the fun really starts!

I recommend you tackle one letter at a time. Before you start to write each letter, take note of the order and direction of the strokes. As you begin writing, you will notice that you are using the strokes from the previous section and building up your letters one stroke at a time.

- Be mindful of the shapes you are making—remember that you want oval shapes.
- Be conscious of your letter slant and try for consistency as you write.
- Remember the pressure and release rule (page 27).
- Check that your nib is correctly placed on the paper.
- Try the different variations or come up with some of your own and then decide which works best for you.
- Make consistency your goal until you are able to make beautiful, graceful letterforms without really thinking too much.

Good luck and have lots of fun with this alphabet section!

Letters of the alphabet

aA

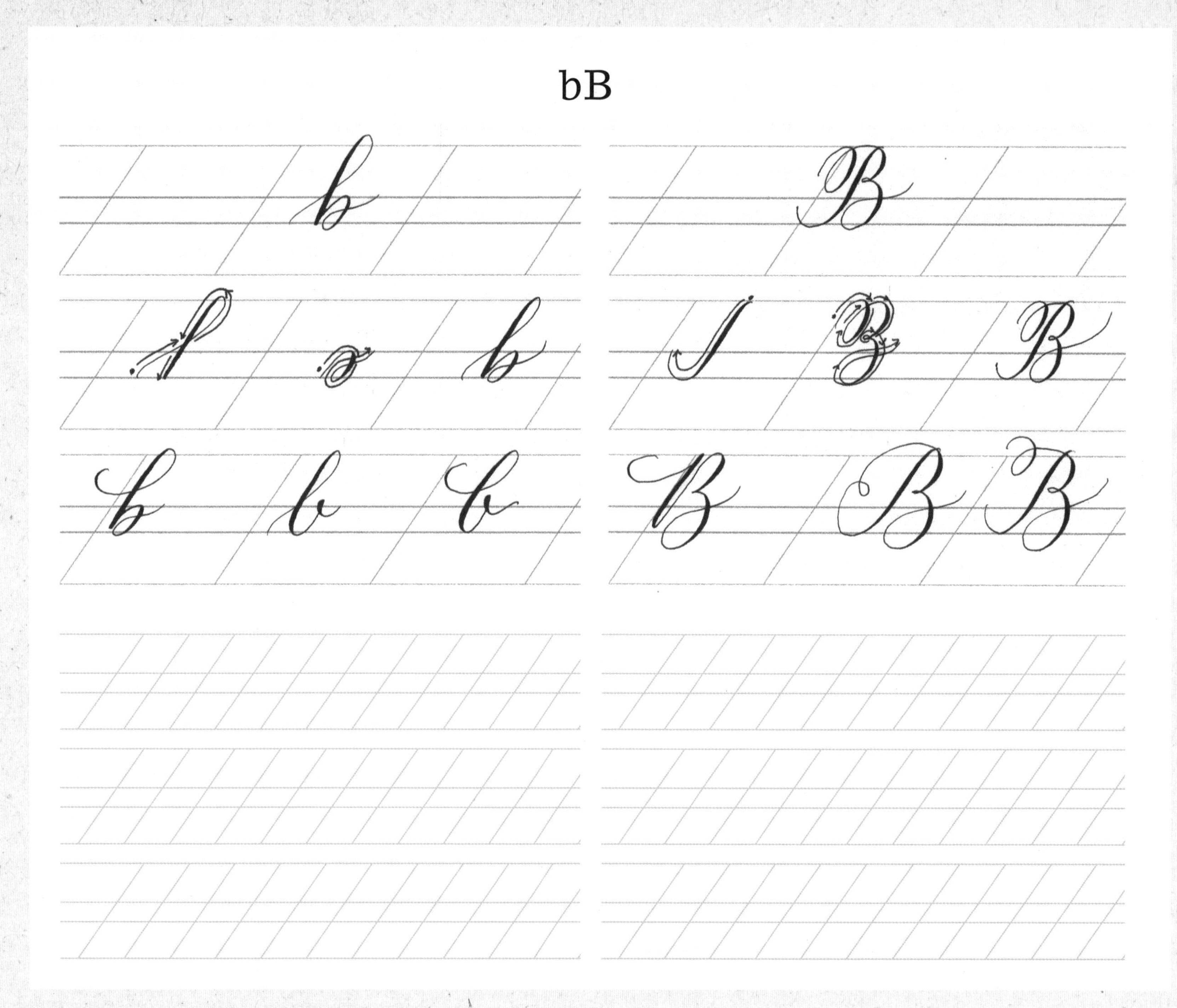
bB

cC

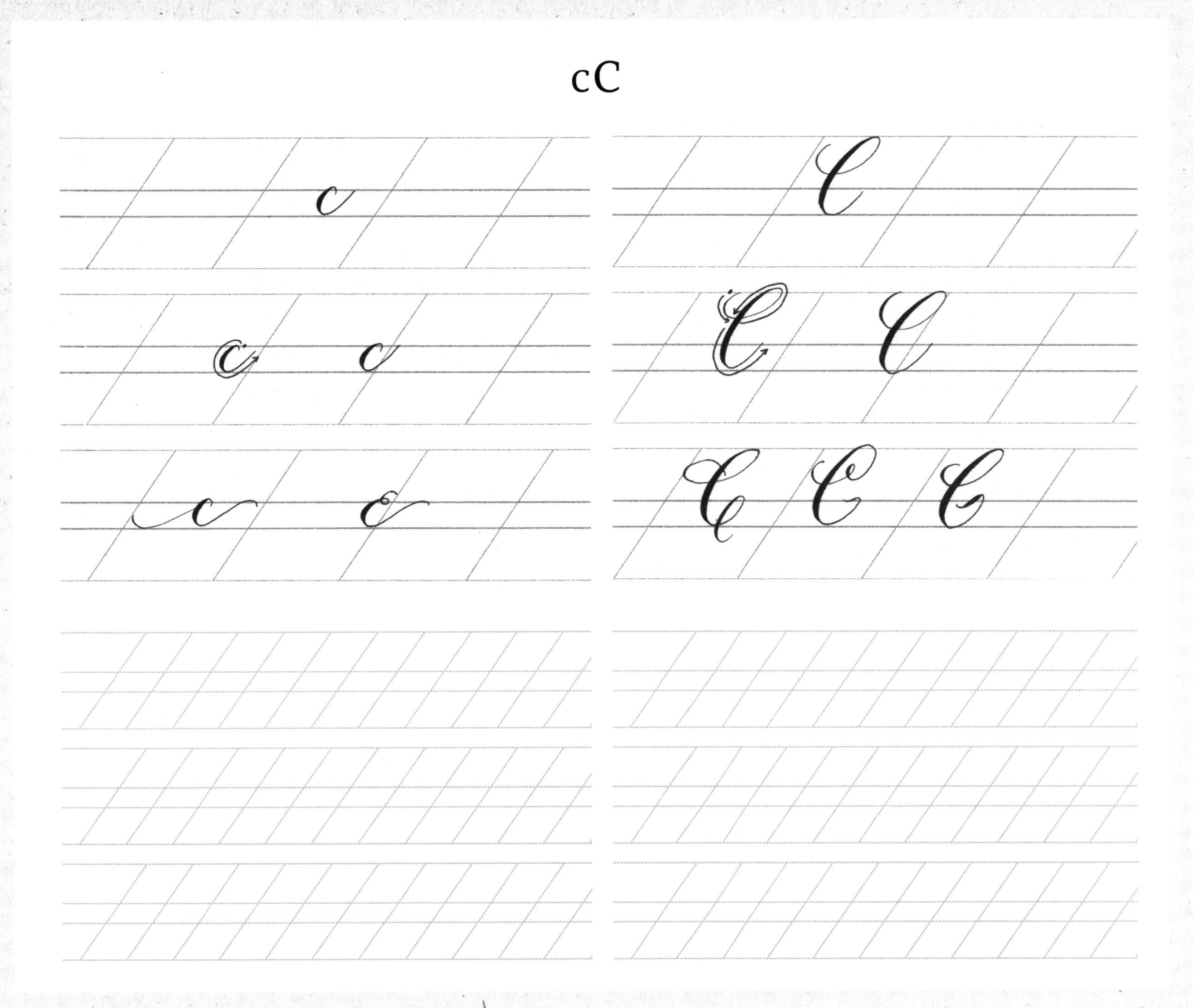

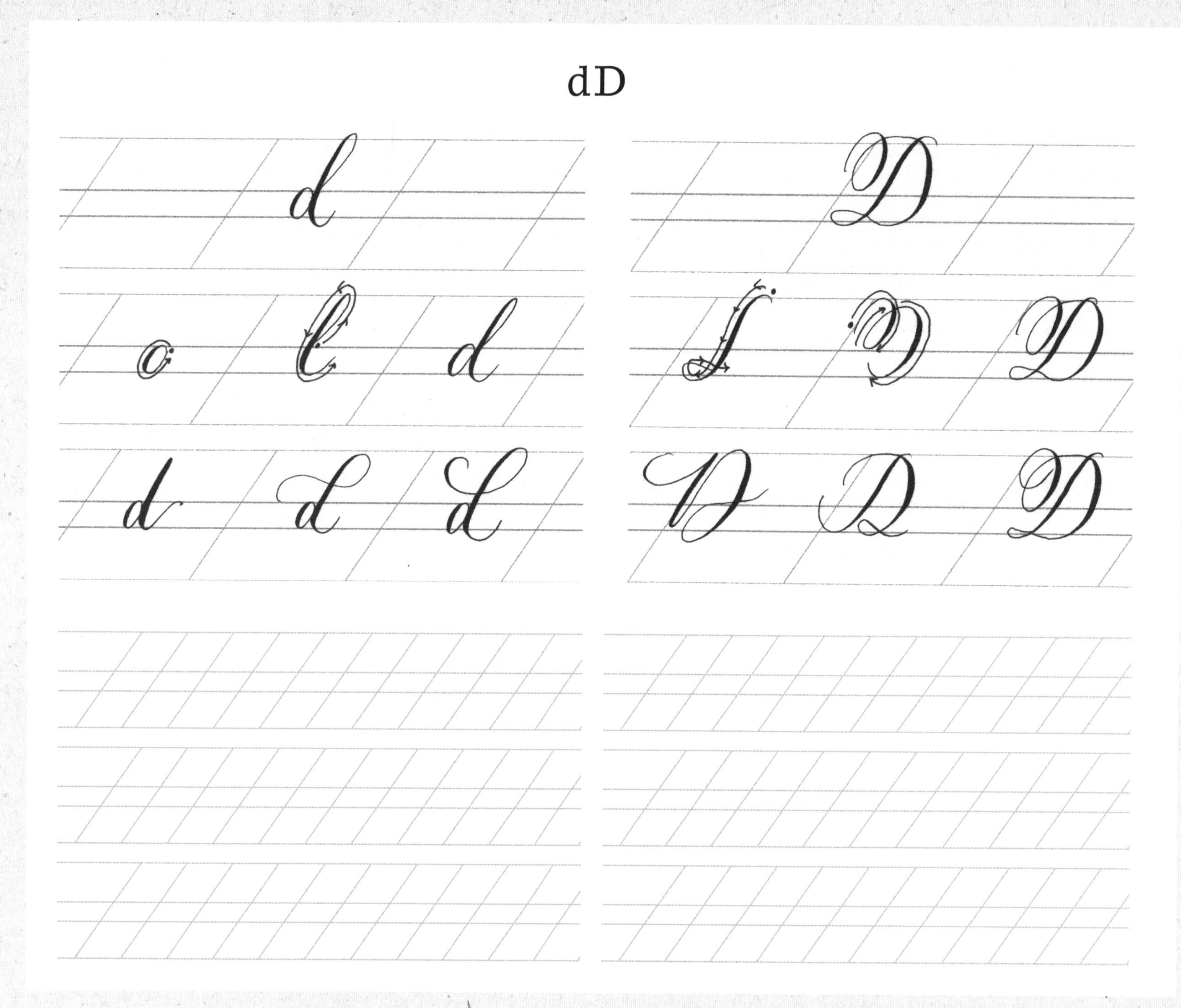
dD

eE

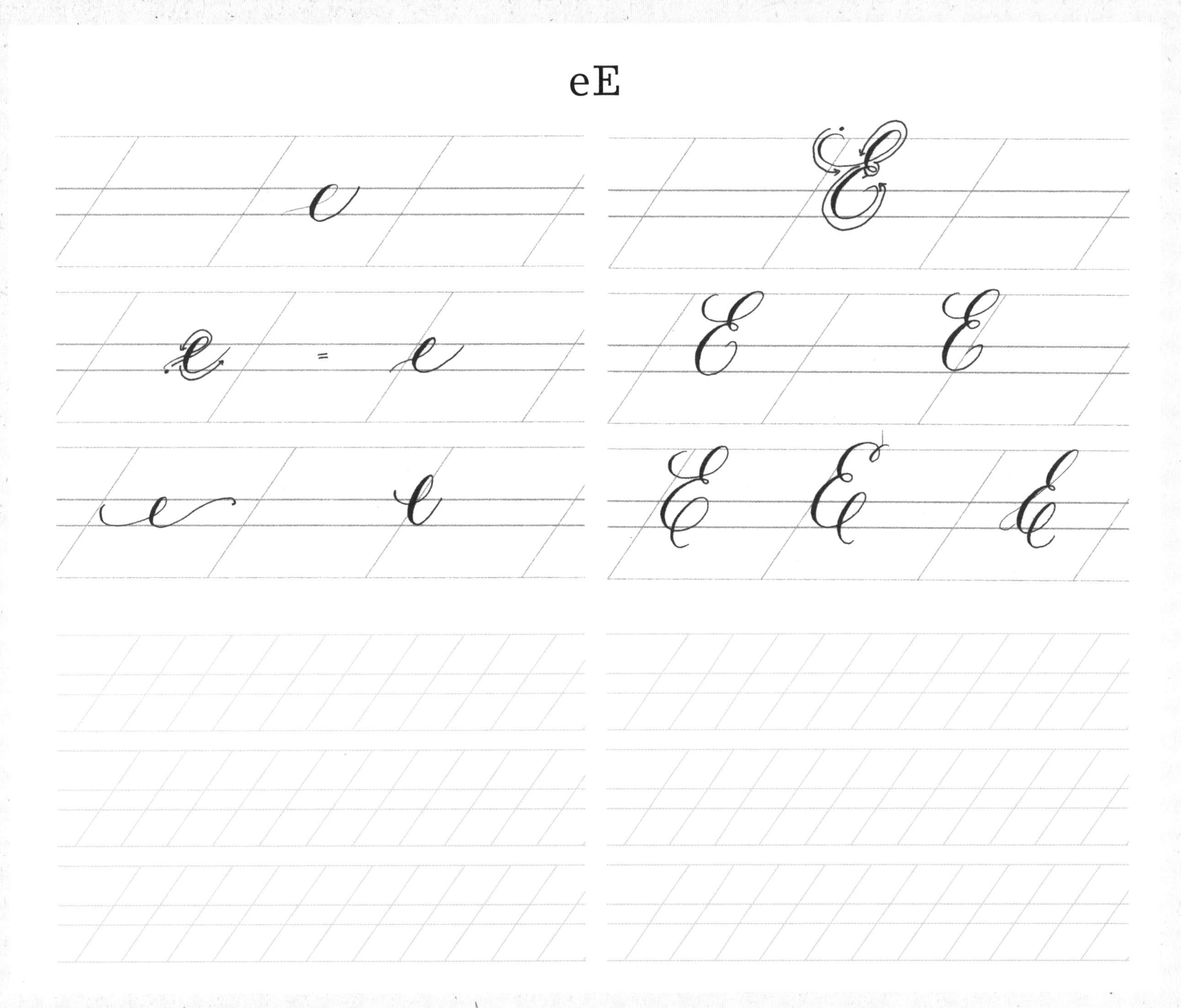

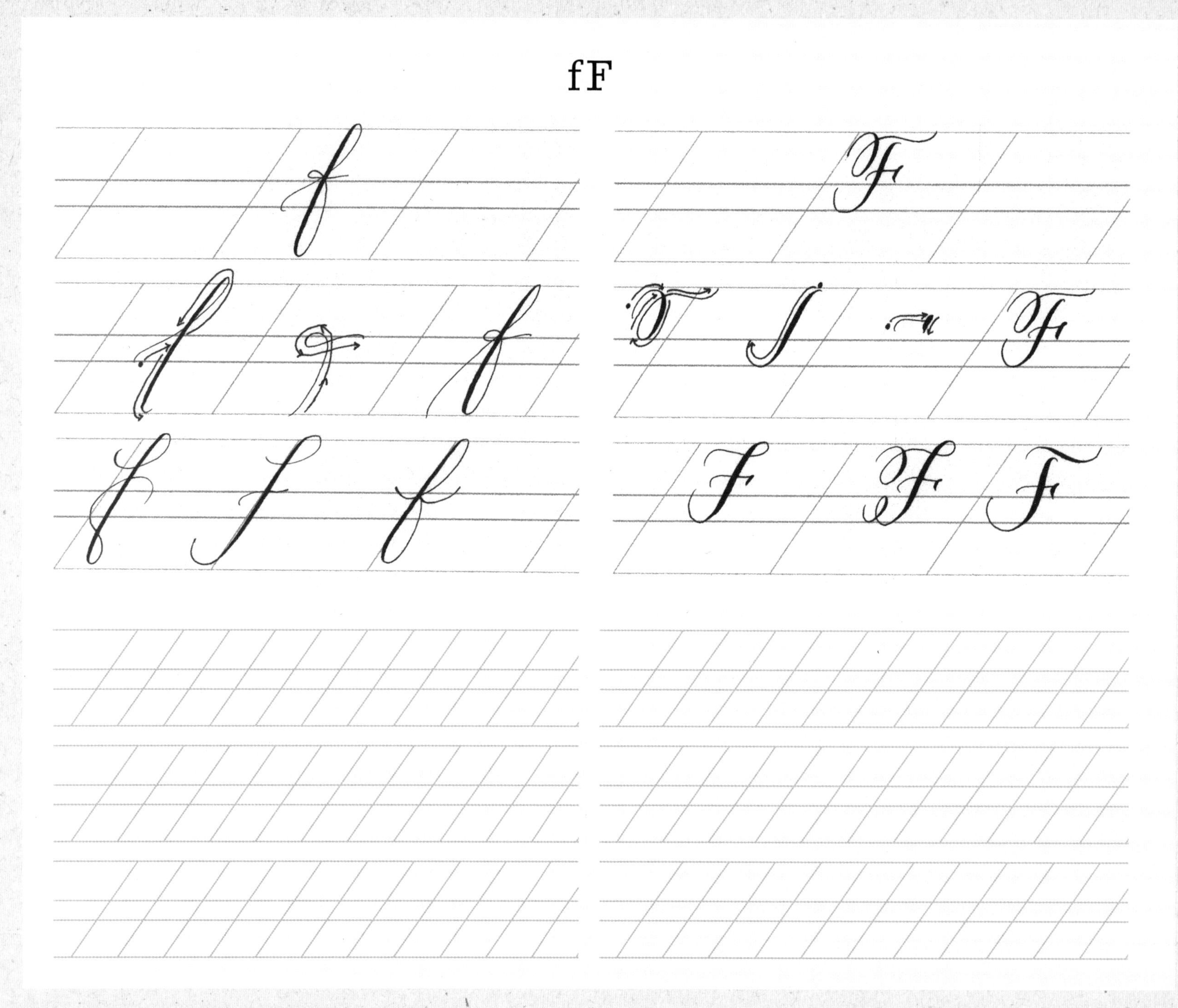
fF

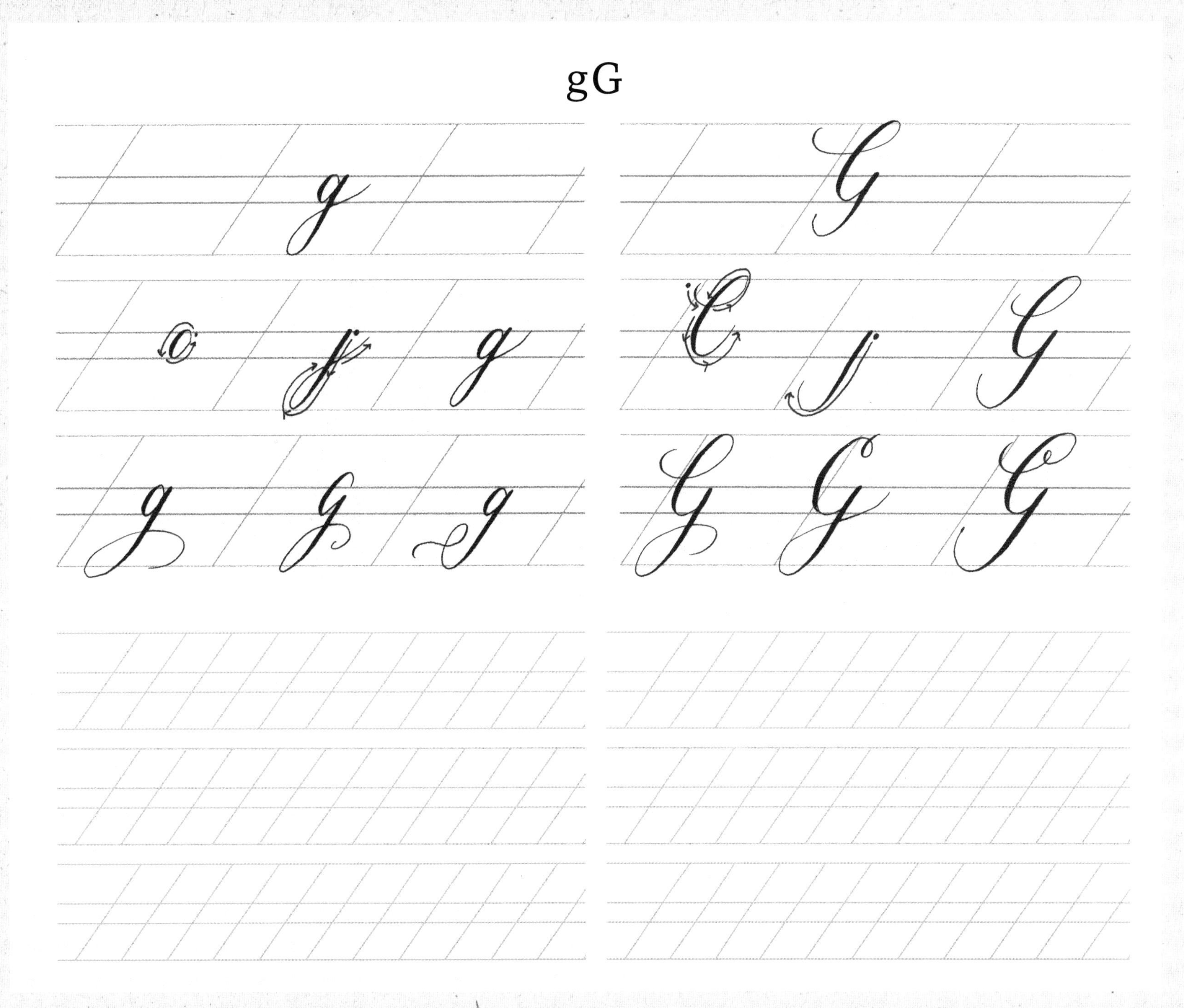
gG

hH

iI

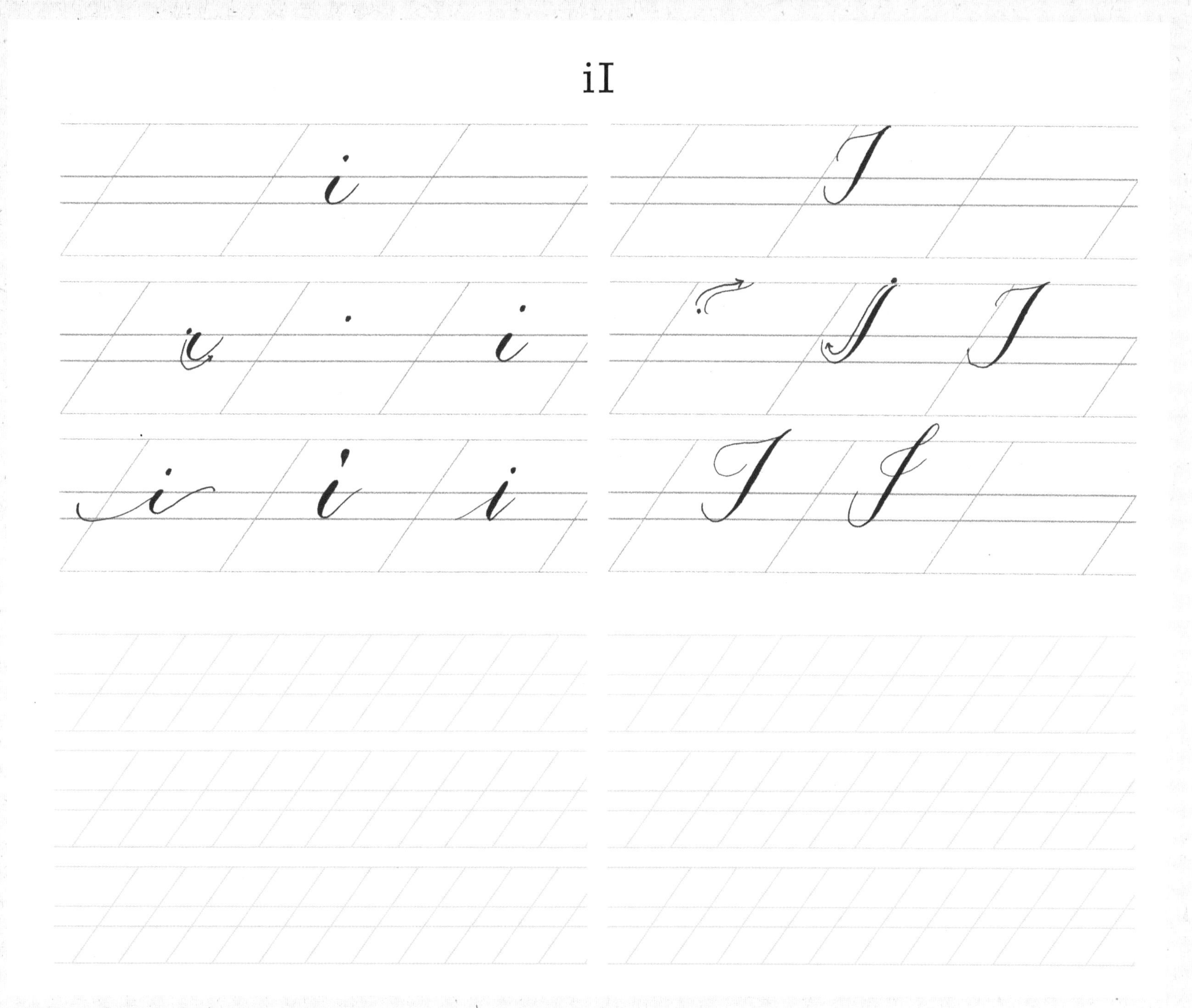

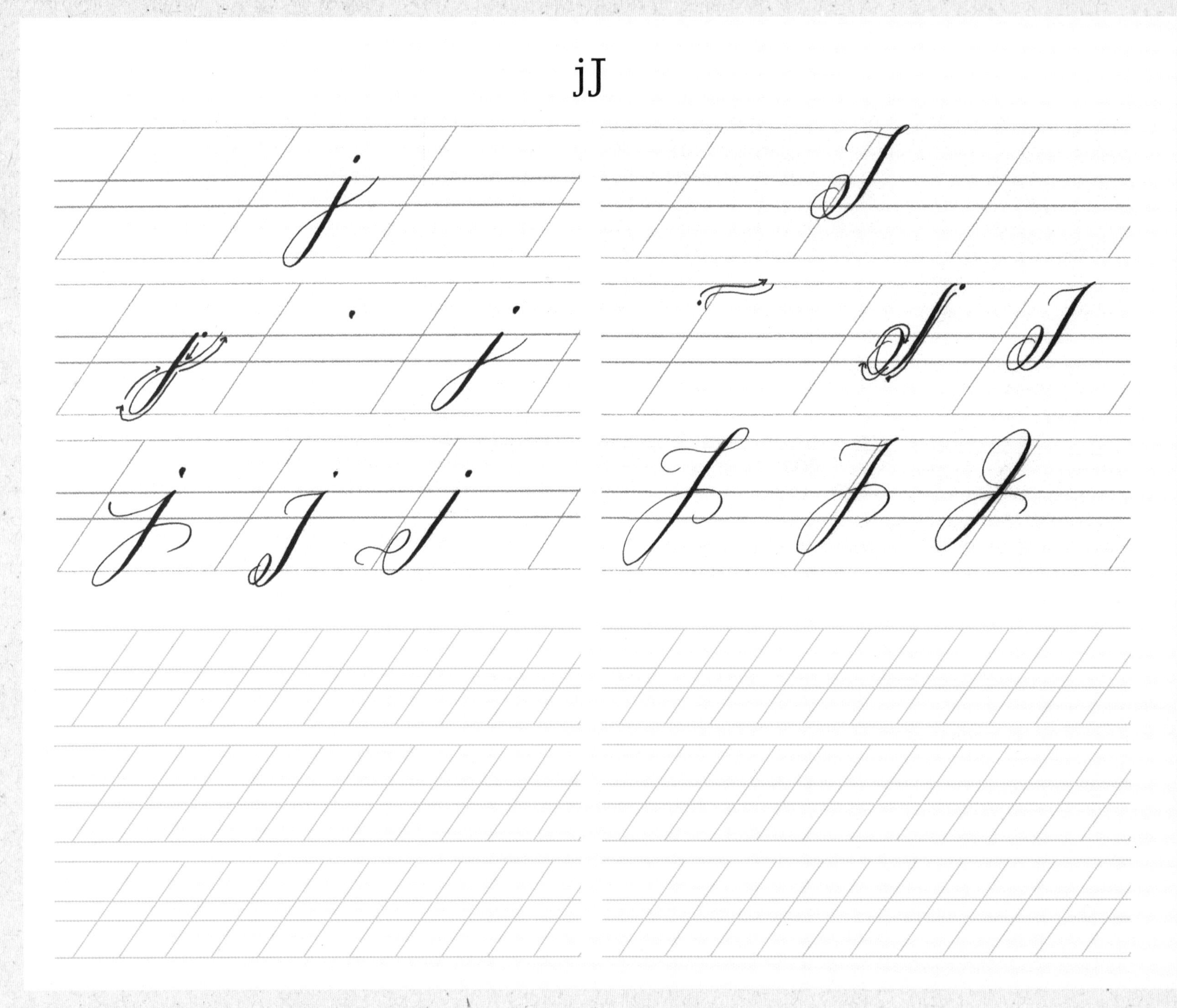
jJ

kK

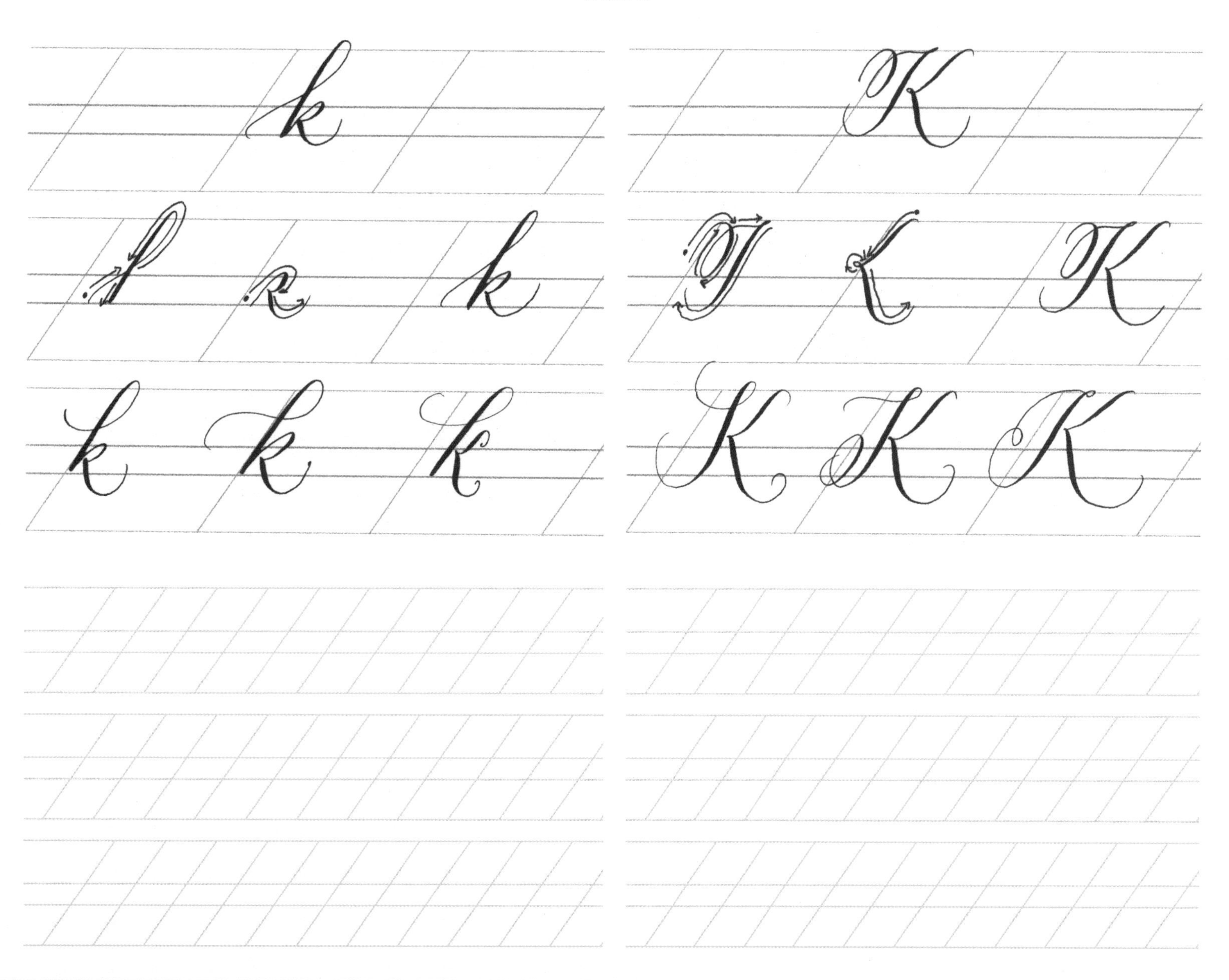

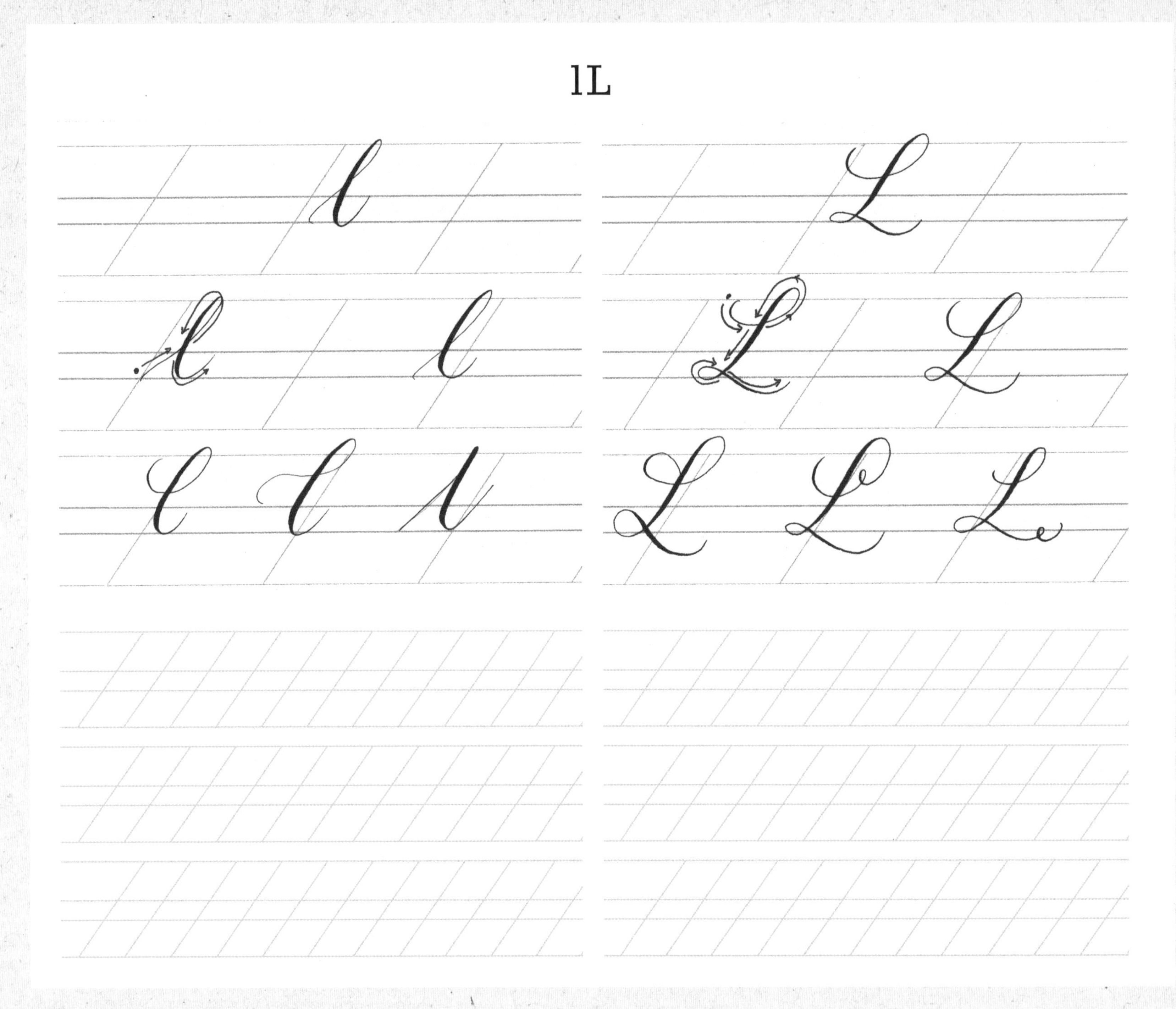
lL

mM

nN

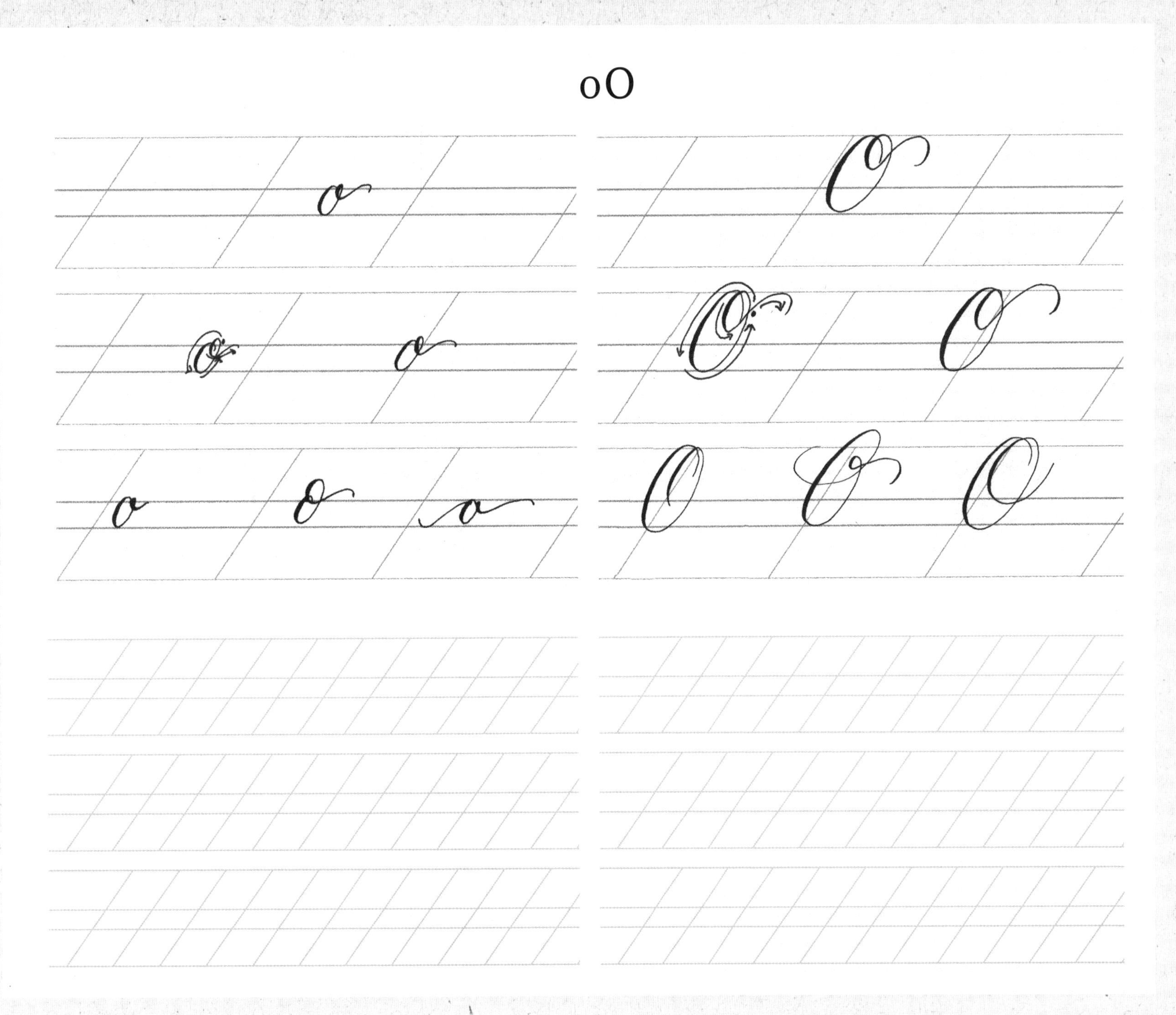
oO

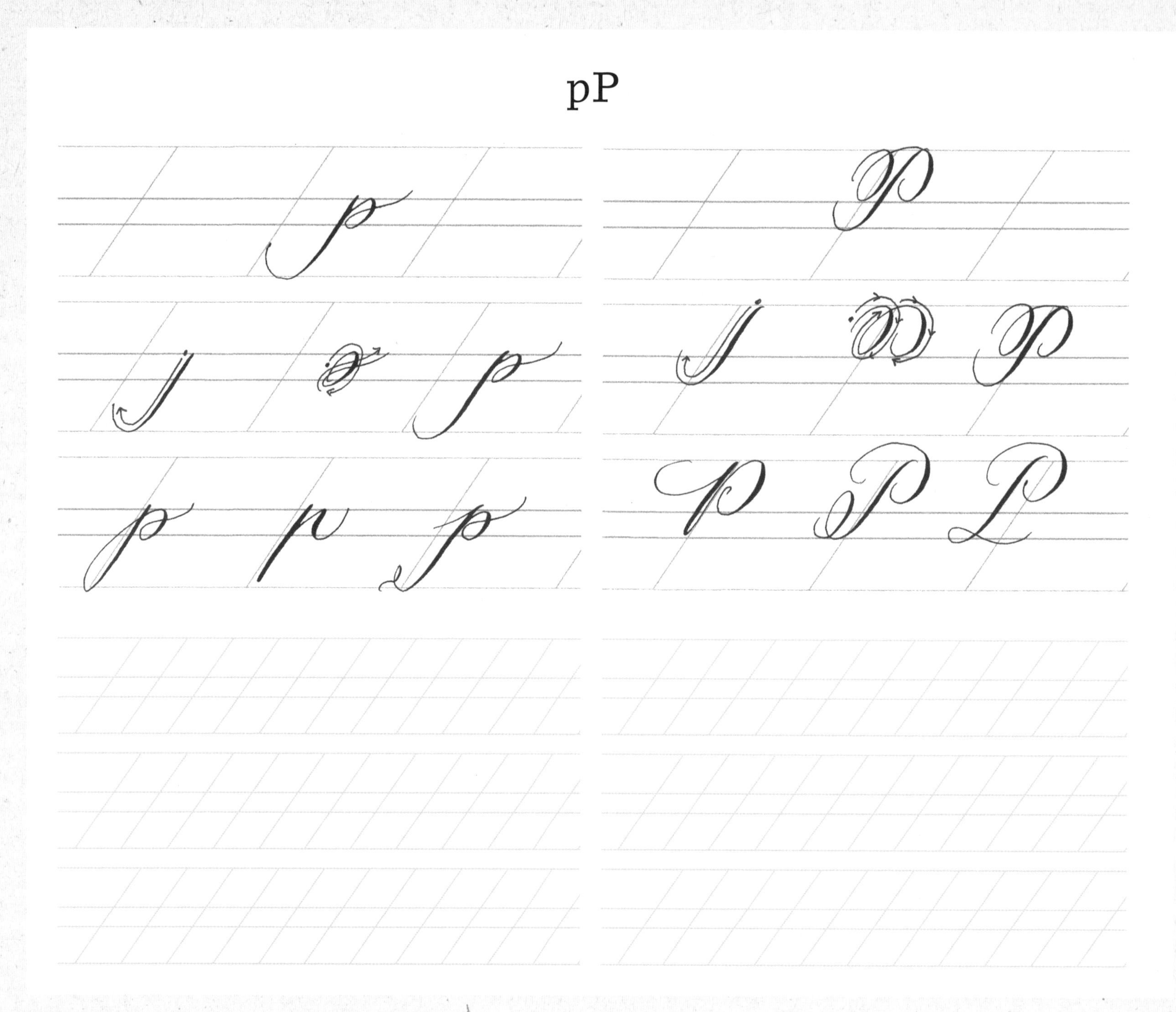
pP

qQ

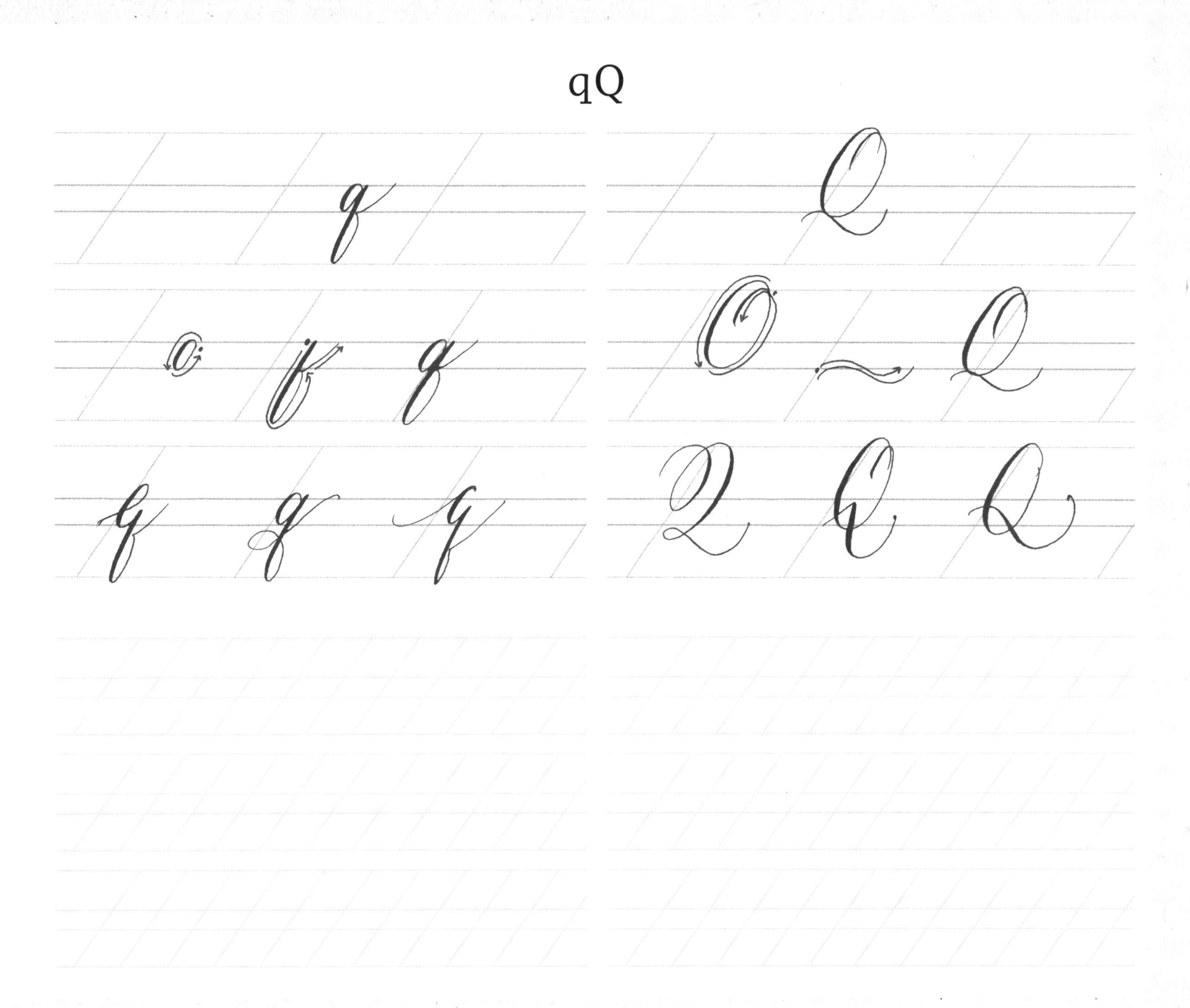

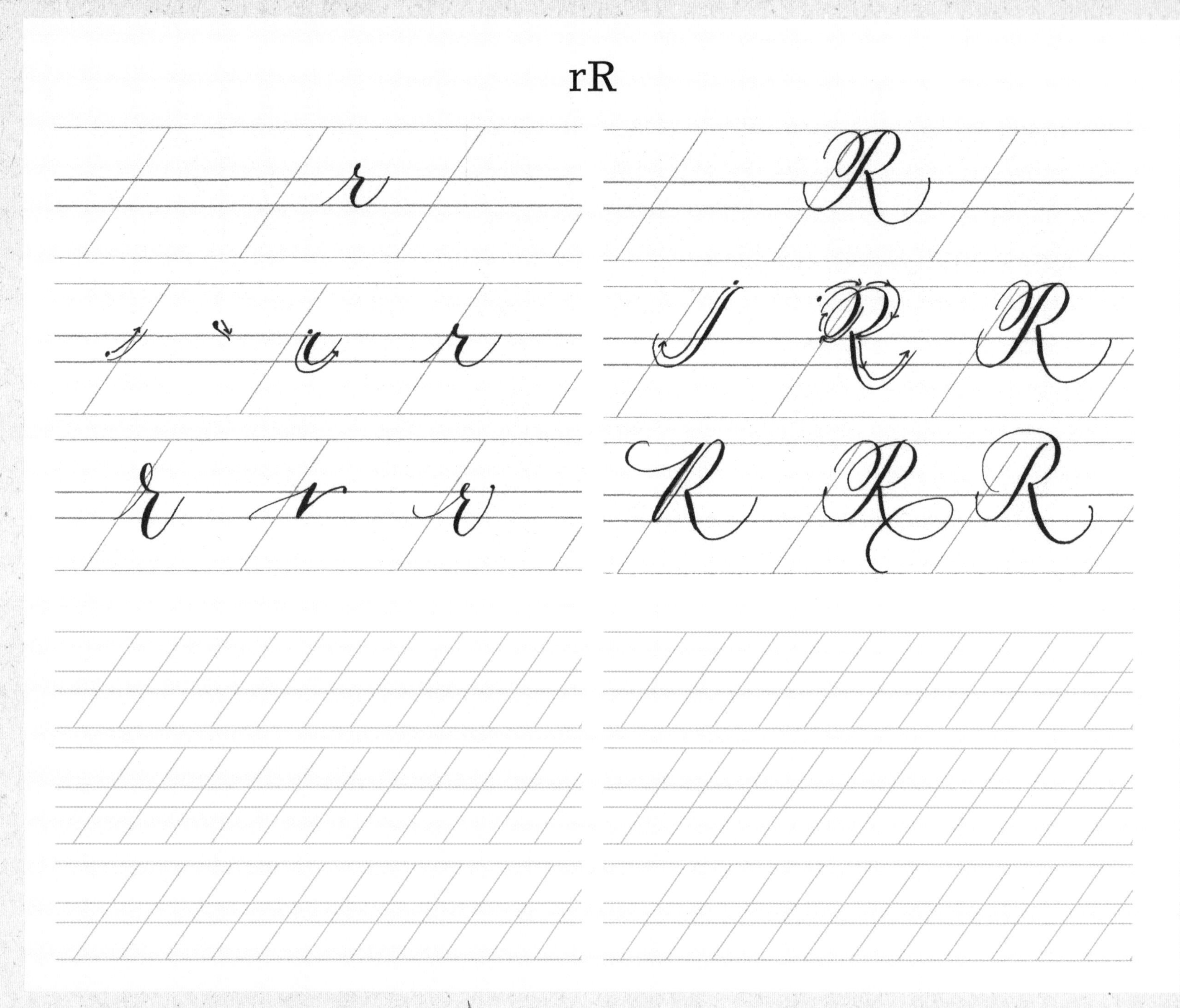
rR

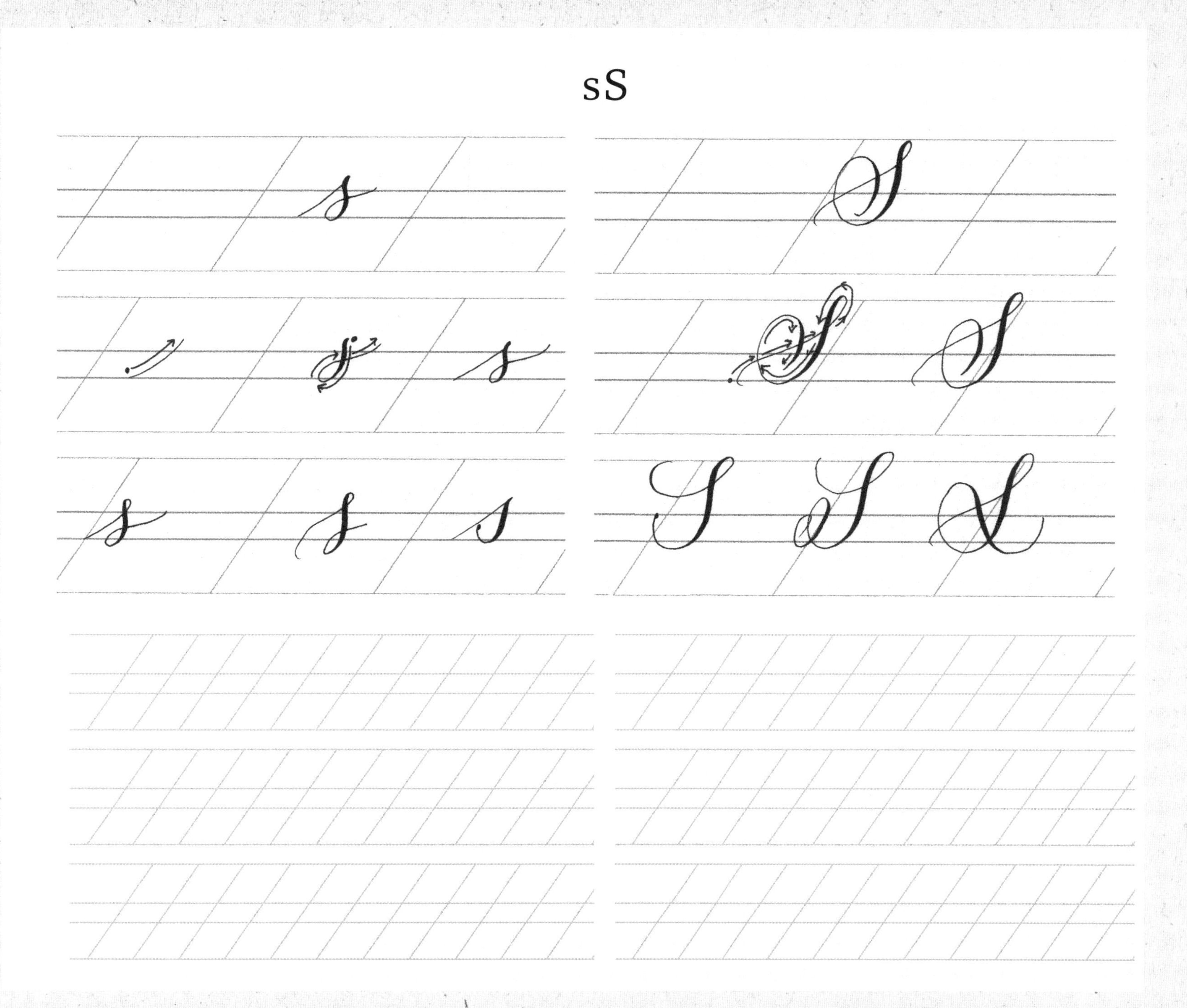
sS

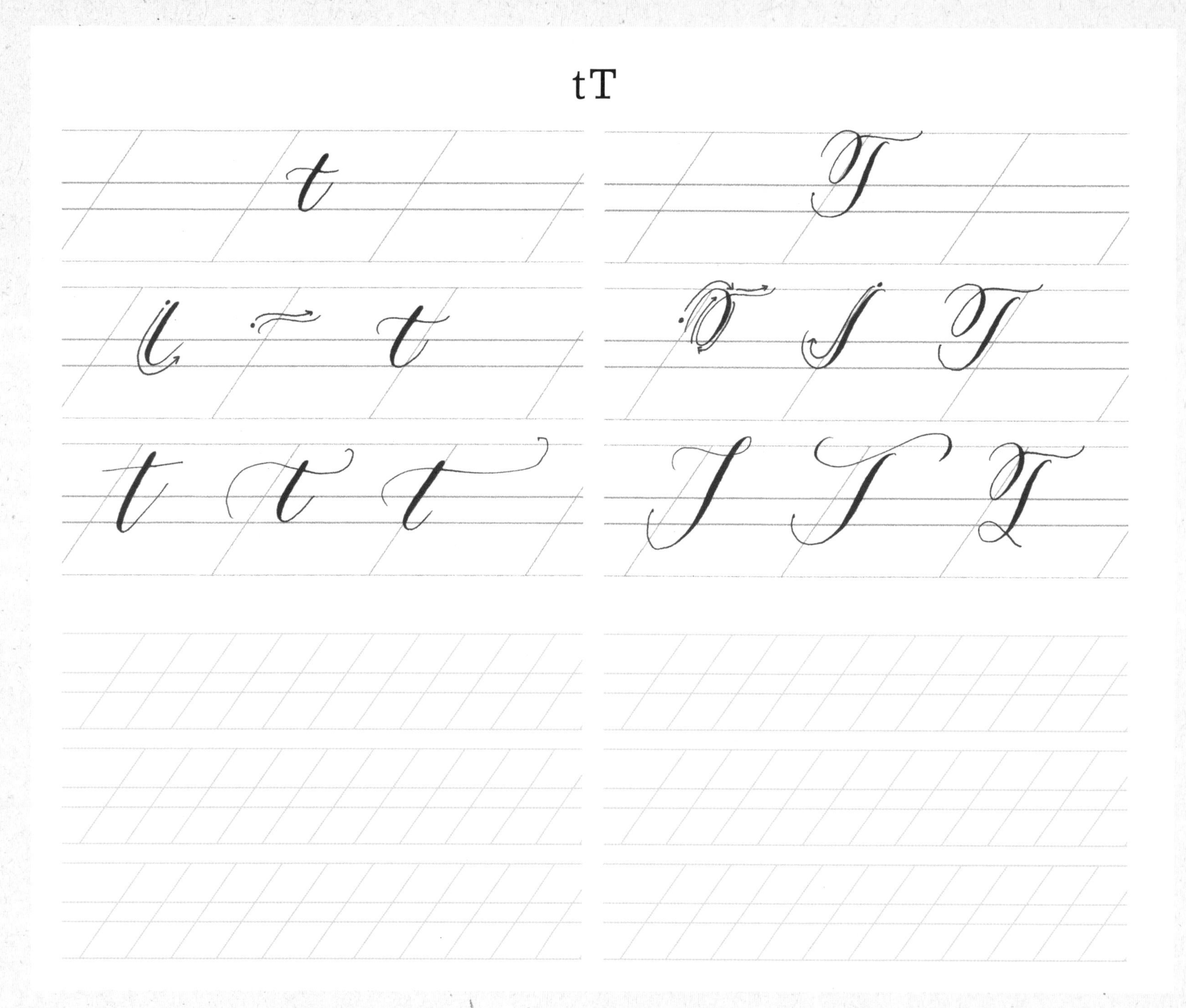
tT

uU

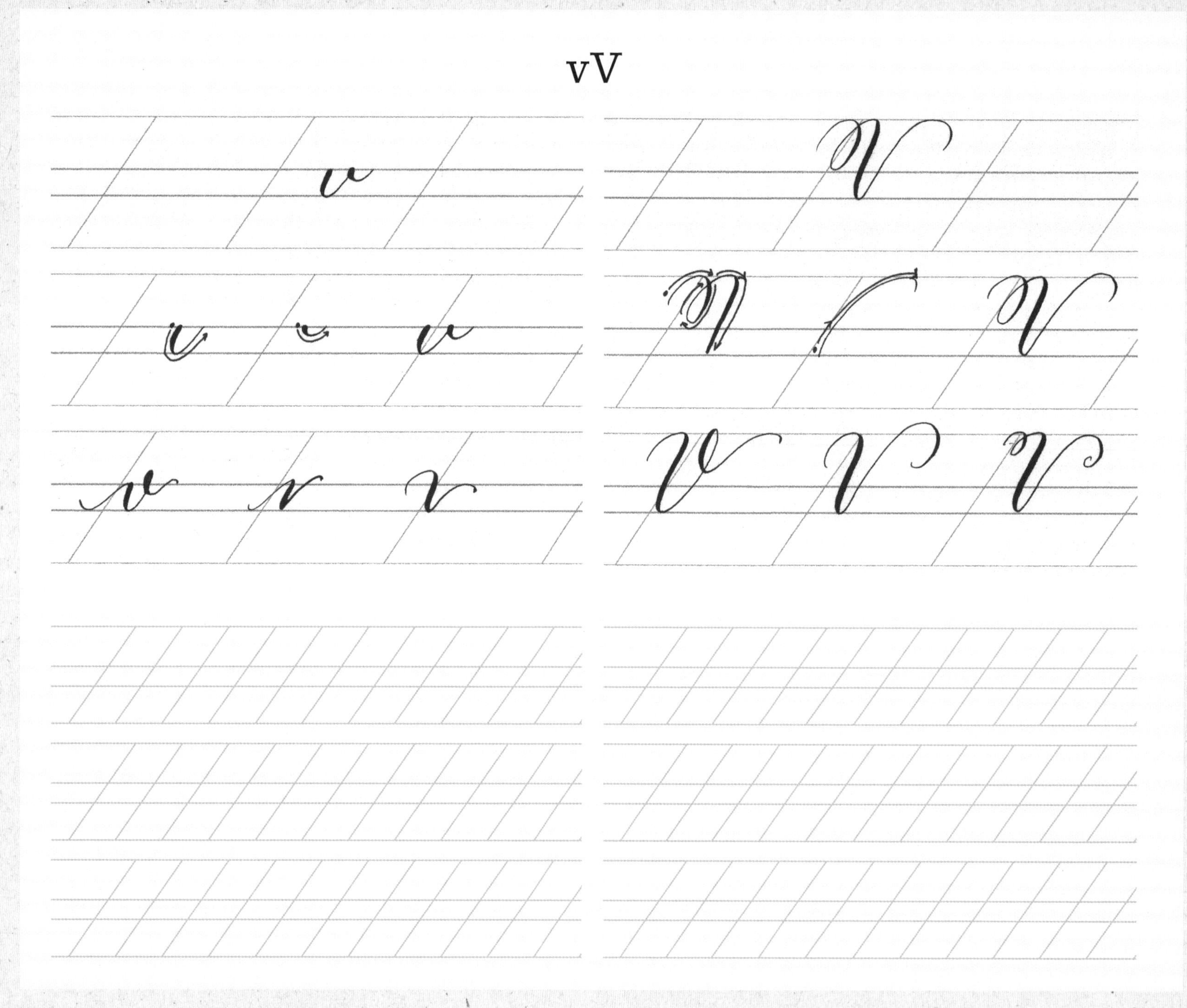
vV

wW

xX

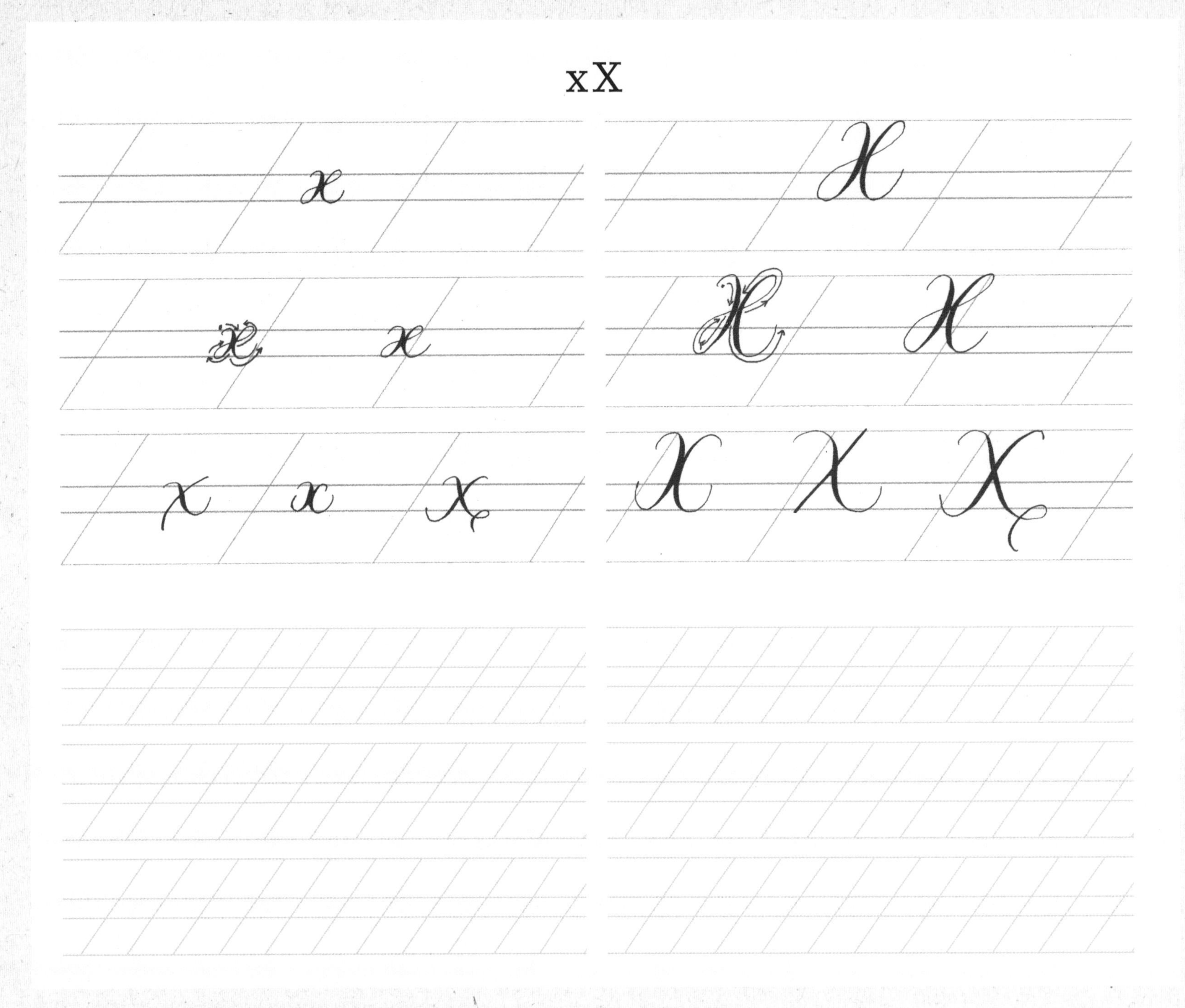

yY

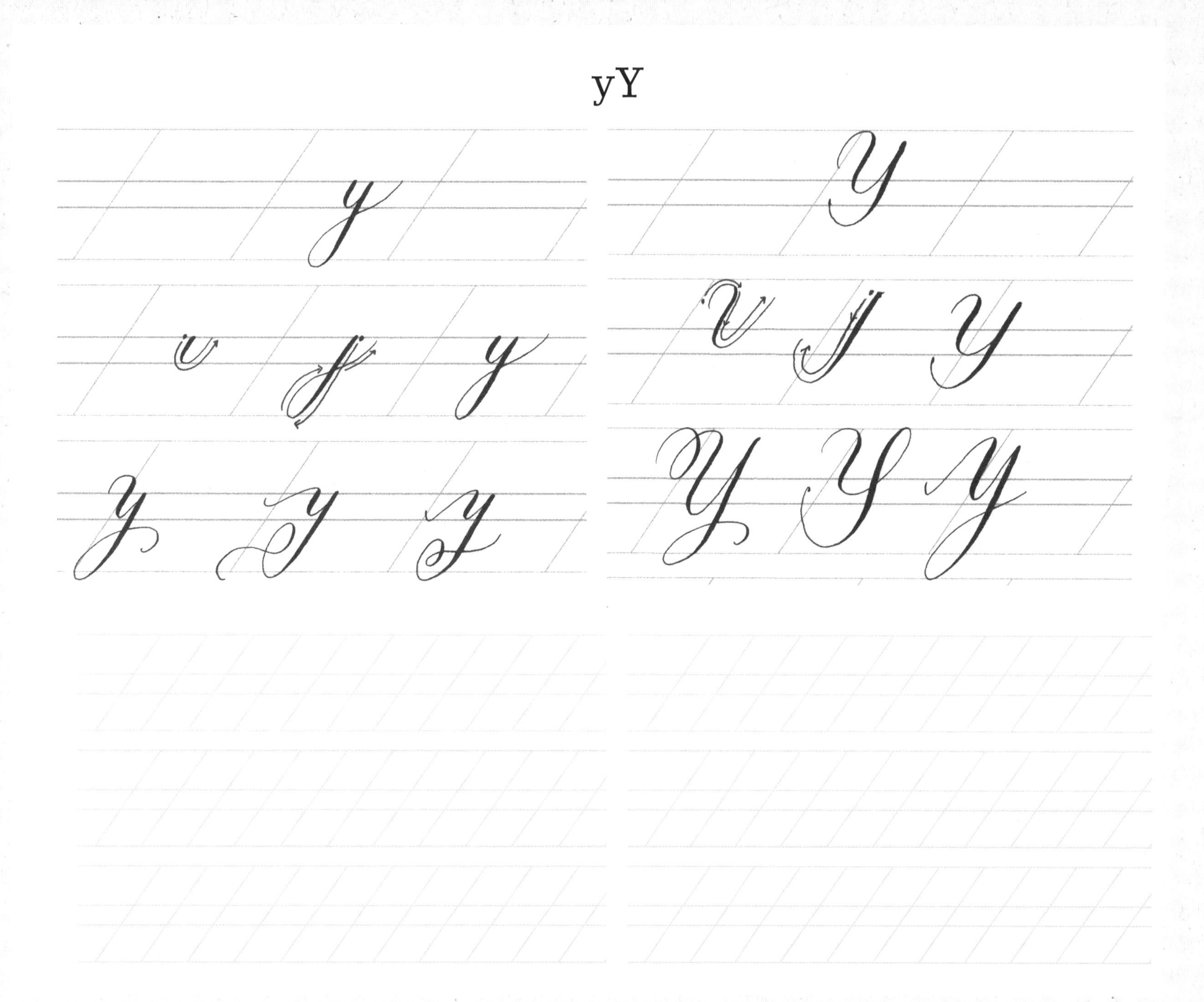

zZ

Accents, special characters and numbers

å â à ä é è ë å ø æ

ó ö ú ü ñ ¿ ¡

1 2 3 4 5 6 7 8 9 0

Taking it up a notch

THE WORLD OF COLOUR

Once you are feeling confident with your lettering, you can start introducing colour. This is where your own sense of style comes into play, and you will find that many of the creative projects in this book use colour to great effect.

There are a variety of ways to add colour to your calligraphy, and in this section I will give a brief outline of my favourite supplies and how to use them.

You will also find the following tools useful when working with colour:

Paintbrush: This is useful for mixing colours and applying paint to the underside of your nib. I like a size 2 round brush, which will also come in handy if you want to try your hand at brush calligraphy.

Pipette/water dropper: Having one of these will enable you to add just the right amount of water when working with colour.

Mixing jars/mixing palette: A few small glass jars are useful for mixing and storing colours. Alternatively, use a mixing palette.

Cutting mat and cutting knife: When it comes to cutting card and paper for your calligraphy projects, a cutting mat and cutting knife will prove useful additions.

Gouache

An opaque water-based paint, gouache comes in small tubes and is widely available from all good art shops and online retailers. There is a huge array of colours to choose from, and as with most calligraphy supplies, it is advisable to use well-known brands for best results.

With gouache you can blend colours together. So if you start off with the primary colours and some black and white, almost any colour will be at your fingertips.

Gouache straight from the tube is too thick to write with, so you need to mix it with water until you have the right consistency.

1. Squeeze a small amount of gouache into a glass jar or mixing palette.

2. Add some drops of water with a dropper or pipette, and mix with a paintbrush until you have a consistency similar to cream.

3. Either dip your nib in the jar or paint the underside of the nib with the gouache.

4. Test the gouache to see if you have the right consistency. If the gouache doesn't flow through the nib, it is still too thick; add a few more drops of water. If, on the other hand, the gouache runs off the nib and the colour is transparent (on the paper), you will need to add more gouache.

Once you have the right consistency, you are ready to write. Sometimes I will just dip the very tip of the nib in my water to start the flow. Gouache will dry on your nib fairly quickly, which can hinder the flow, so regularly clean your nib as you write. Experiment with different colours on different-coloured papers.

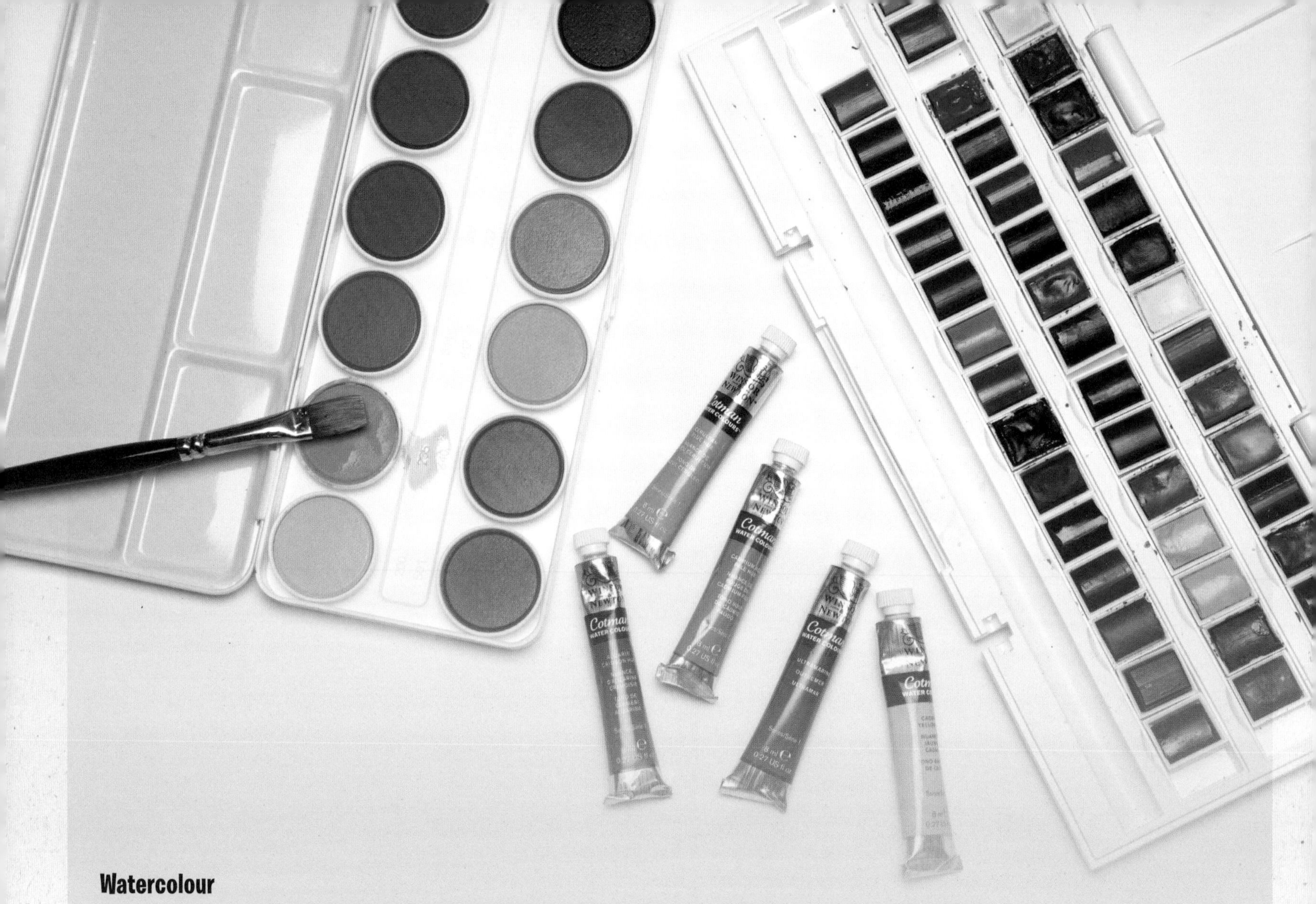

Watercolour

This can be used to great effect. You can purchase watercolour in tubes, small blocks or pans, and as with gouache, there is a huge array of colours to choose from. Add some water to your blocks or pans and mix with a brush to achieve the right consistency. If you are using watercolour in a tube, squeeze a small amount into a dish or jar, and mix with water as for gouache.

Watercolour has a wonderful translucent quality, which can produce stunning effects. As you write, the colour will change, becoming more translucent. You can add a new colour to your nib as it runs out of paint; this will blend with the original colour, giving a lovely natural look when the different colours merge together.

ARE YOU LEFT-HANDED?

I have found that left-handed people are sometimes worried that they will not be able to master calligraphy, but there are in fact many talented left-handed calligraphers.

It is my experience that most left-handed people get on better with a straight pen holder rather than an oblique pen holder, and find it easier to adopt a more upright style of writing. Experiment and see which feels more natural to you.

If you are an under-writer, which means that your hand will be under the base line of your writing and your wrist will be straight, you may prefer to turn your page in a clockwise direction up to 90 degrees. By doing this you are giving your arm and elbow room to travel across the page, which will make writing easier.

If you are an over-writer, you will be writing from above the base line, your hand will be curled over and the pen holder is pointing away from you. If this is how you write, I confess it can be a little more challenging. For you, the thicker stroke will be an upward stroke away from you with even pressure. The hairline stroke will be the downward stroke coming towards you with no pressure. You will be drawing your letters from the bottom upwards rather than from the top down.

WORDS AND SENTENCES

You are now ready to progress to writing words and sentences. This can be challenging at first, but follow these tips and with practice you will soon improve.

Pace

When you start with words, it can be very tempting to quicken your pace and revert to your normal writing speed. If you do this, you are likely to lose the contrast between your thick and thin strokes, and you may stop forming your letters correctly. Try to develop a slow, rhythmic pace.

Connections

Pay attention to the connections between your letters. How you connect one letter to the next can dramatically affect how your words will look. Your connecting strokes will look better if they all have consistent angles.

Spacing

Pay attention to your spacing. Try to aim for even, consistent spacing between your letters. To begin with, write a letter and take your exit stroke to the midway point before starting the next letter. By doing this, you should end up with even spacing.

Letterforms

Keep an eye on your letterforms, making sure you continue to form them correctly, building them up stroke by stroke. Be aware of your slant and angles too.

PRACTICE MAKES PROGRESS

As with anything, in order to make good progress you will need to dedicate some time to practise. By practising the same strokes and letterforms, you will develop muscle memory and remember not only what each stroke looks like, but also how it feels to draw it. This in turn will ultimately enable you to make consistently beautiful strokes without giving them very much thought at all.

So practice is your key to progress. It is also important to make your practice sessions productive so that you get the most out of them.

Plan and focus: Plan your practice sessions. How long are you going to practise for? What are you going to practise? Short sessions of 20 minutes are fine, but make every minute count. Focus on the job in hand.

Use the right tools: Using the right tools will help you with your progress. If the ink bleeds on the paper because you're not using a decent paper or your nib is past its sell-by date, you will soon become frustrated and your progress will be hindered.

Be productive: Set yourself mini goals and every so often stop and critique your work. Analyse what went well and what you could improve on. It can sometimes be useful to date your practice sessions too, so you can look back and see your progress over time.

Make it enjoyable: Make your practice sessions fun. Mix things up a little so you don't get jaded. You could write in bright pink, use some coloured paper, write out a favourite motivational quote, or the lyrics to your favourite song.

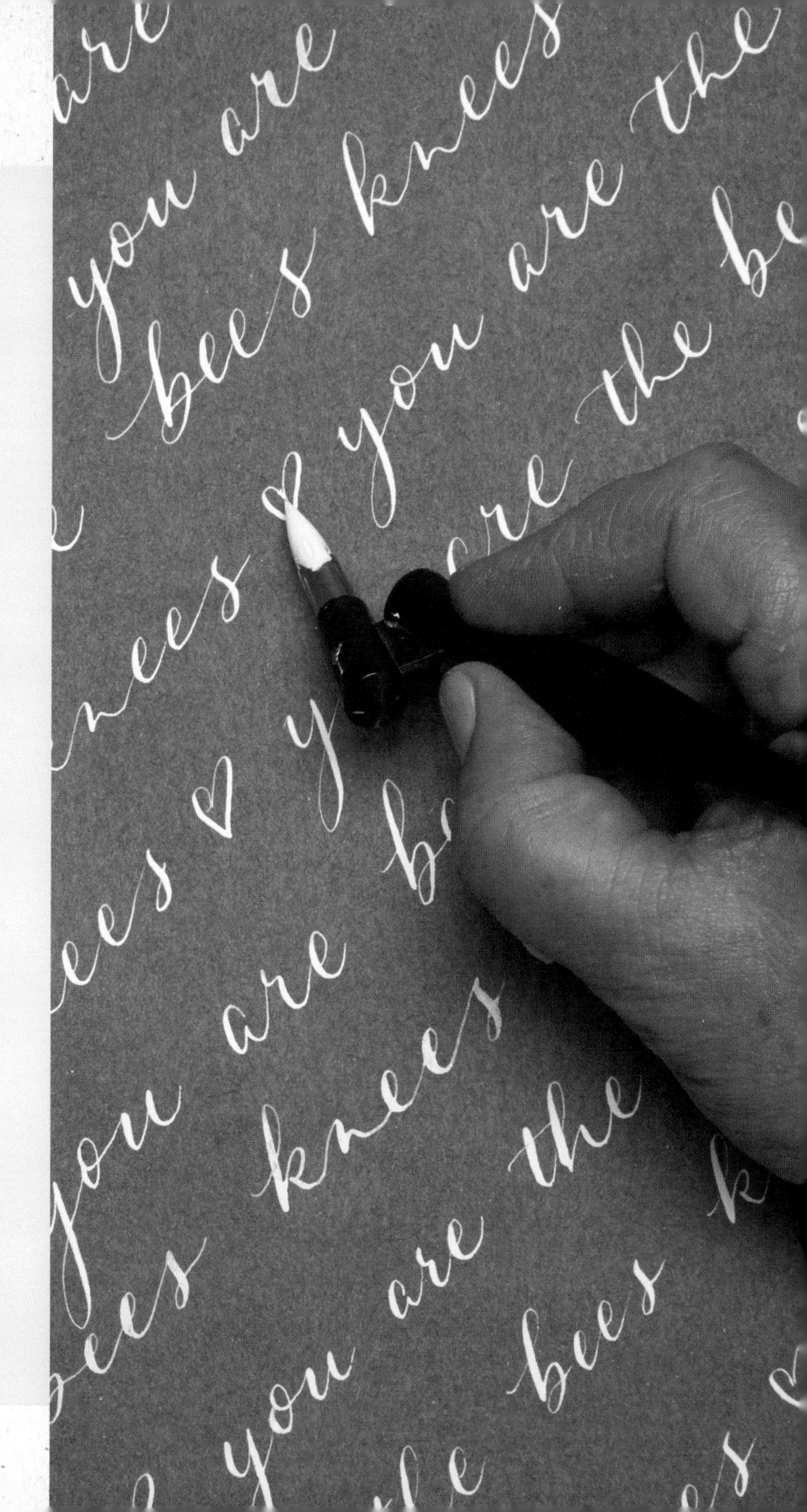

Let's flourish

My guess is that once you have mastered the basics, you will be eager to add a flourish or two.

Everyone who is interested in calligraphy—myself included—is both captivated and enchanted by how the master penmen can flourish their work so effortlessly and beautifully. Adding flourishes is indeed great fun, but it's not as easy as it looks and can take some time to master. As with anything, with some knowledge and some practice you too will be able to create some fabulous flourishes.

Some flourishing tips

- Practise mastering some simple flourishes in pencil first. If you build some muscle memory, they will soon become natural movements and you will be able to draw them without thinking.
- Imagine how your flourish will look, or 'air draw' it before you actually commit pen to paper.
- Aim to use you whole arm. Keep your arm and elbow off the table surface and glide your hand across the page in smooth, fluid movements.
- Turn the page so you can add weight to the downward part of your flourish.
- It is always advisable to keep it simple. Try not to get too carried away with flourishing. One beautiful flourish is sometimes all that you need.
- Avoid crossing a thick line with another thick line or finishing your flourish abruptly. You want the flourishes to look natural and graceful.
- Aim to cross lines at approximately 90 degrees for visually pleasing flourishes. Flourishes that are parallel to the horizontal can also work well. Think oval and rounded shapes when making loops in your flourishes.

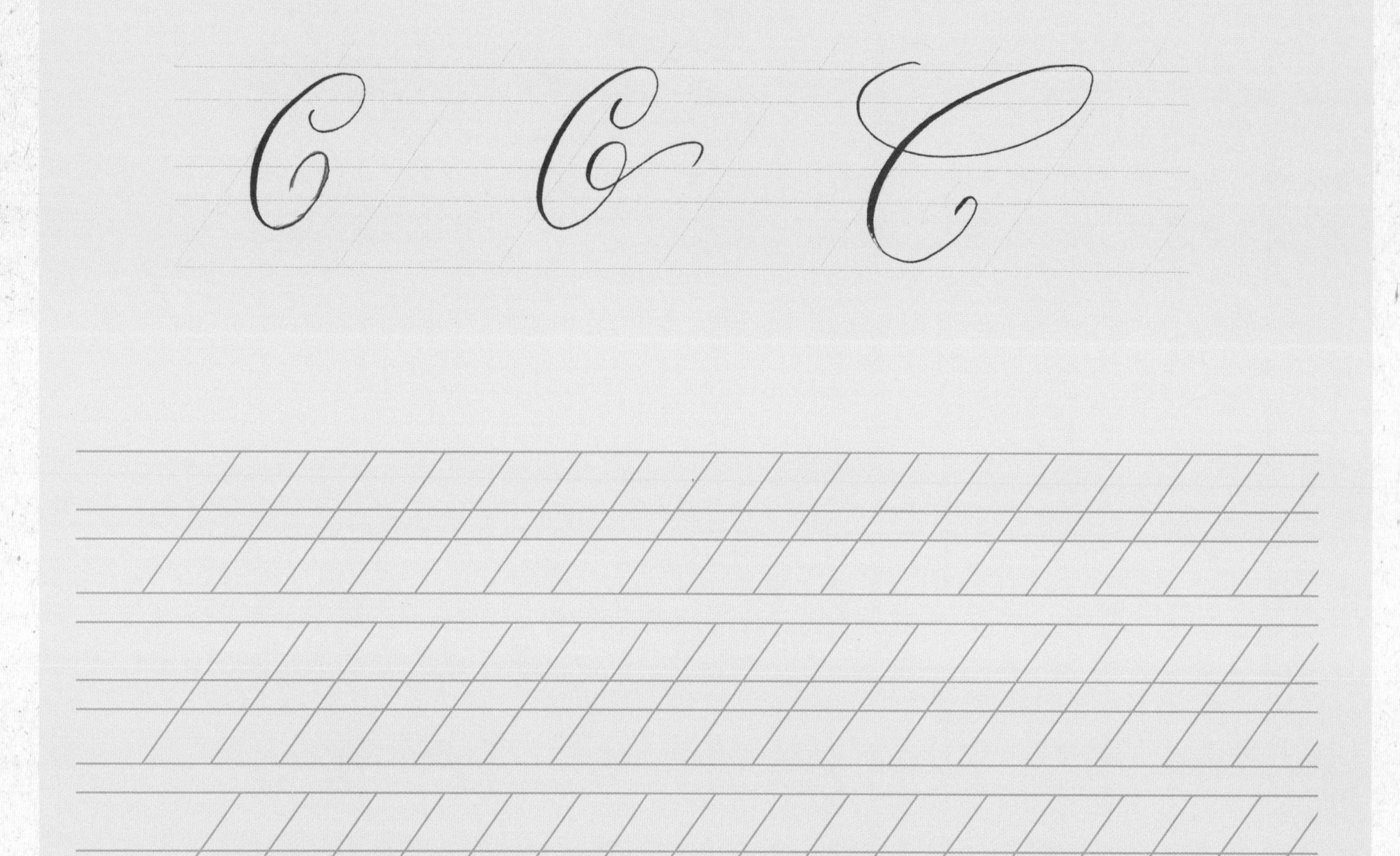

Where to flourish

- Add a flourish at the start of a word or line, and again at the end of a word/line.
- Add a flourish above or below a word.
- Add flourishes to the top of your ascender strokes and to the bottom of the descender strokes. Check the variations in the earlier alphabet section for examples of this.
- Add flourishes to the start or end of your capital letters. Again, you can see examples of this in the alphabet section (see pages 55–64).
- The simple steps below will show you how to start practising your flourishing. Have fun with this and you will soon learn some easy flourishes to add to your calligraphy repertoire.

Congratulations

◀ Write out a word or phrase in pencil, but leave out the ascender and descender loops.

Congratulations

◀ Determine where you can add a flourish using the tips on the previous page to guide you. I have indicated with arrows where there are opportunities to flourish.

▶ Pencil in some simple flourishes, without being too ambitious.

Congratulations

◀ You can choose to embellish further by adding some smaller flourishes and loops.

▶ Once you are happy with your design, go over it with ink.

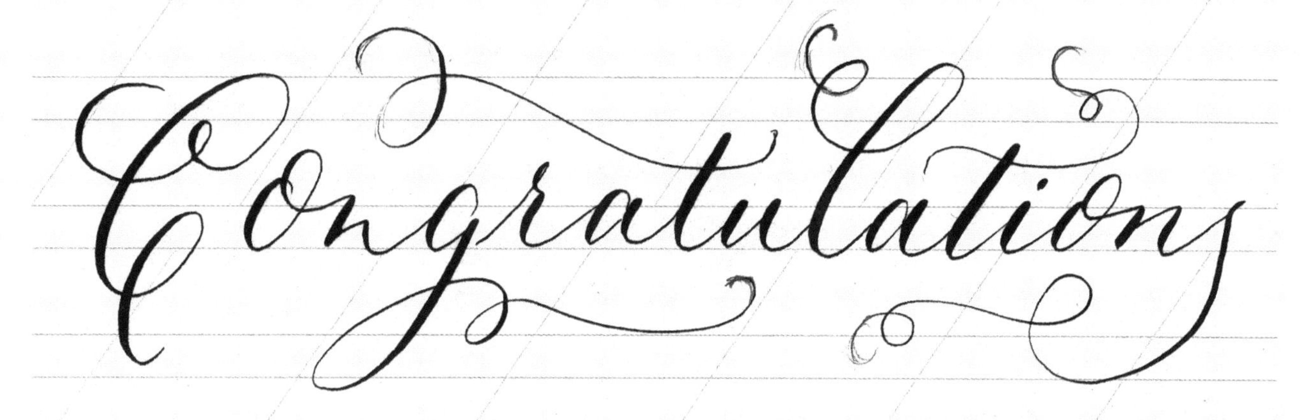

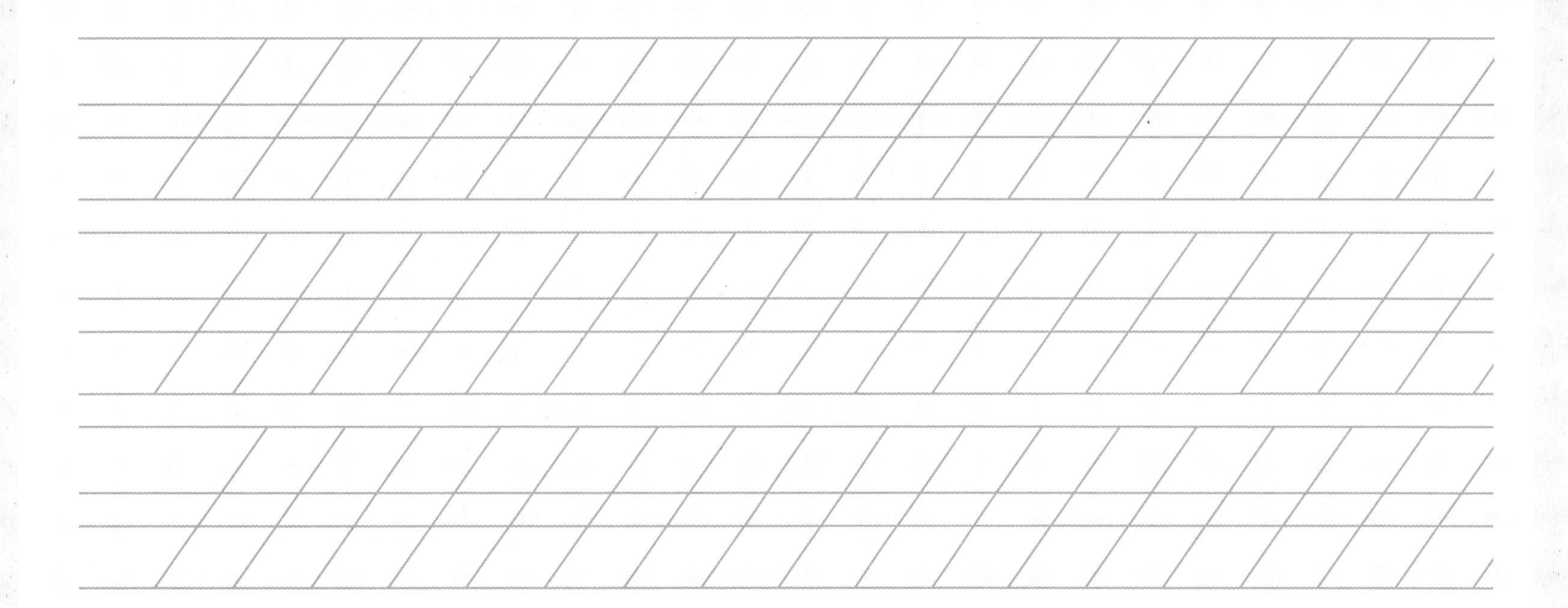

Developing your own style

As you become more confident and experienced, you will undoubtedly start to develop your own lettering style. Play around with spacing and proportions, and notice the effect these have on the overall look. Choose a style you like and feel comfortable with. You may use a different style depending on the project you are working on.

If I am addressing envelopes for a formal invitation, I might choose a style that is evenly spaced and has a more traditional feel. If, on the other hand, I am sending a birthday card to a friend or writing a gift tag for a present, I might adopt a more loose and playful style. A looser and more upright script will have a more contemporary feel to it. Just bear in mind that you are aiming for consistency on any given project.

To try

Take a word—such as 'hello'—and practise writing it in different ways.

Slanted

hello

Upright

hello

Extra large

hello

Mini

hello

Sharp and tight

hello

Loose

hello

Loose and bouncy

hello

Extra bold

hello

Flourished

Light and whimsical

Troubleshooting

From time to time, your calligraphy may not go quite as well as you would like. There is usually a simple explanation. The following points cover the main problems you may encounter.

Shaky upstroke

This can be a common problem when you are first learning calligraphy. As you become more experienced, the wobbles should soon disappear. Remember to keep your whole arm relaxed, and aim for smooth, fluid movements.

Nib snagging and ink splatters

If your nib is catching on the upstrokes and causing a mini ink explosion, there may be a few explanations. First, check your paper. If the paper you are using is too rough or textured, the tines could be catching on the upstrokes, which will cause the splatters. Try changing the paper. Alternatively, apply less pressure, especially as you do your upstrokes, and check the direction of the nib. Remember, you are aiming for the nib to glide gently over the paper and be pointing in the direction it is moving. And lastly, check your nib carefully—it may simply be a case that it is time to buy a new one.

Ink flow

All calligraphers can experience problems with ink flow at times. Check the consistency of the ink you are using—it may be too thick. This can often be the case when working with gouache, in which you may need to add a few drops of water. Alternatively, just try dipping the very tip of the nib into some water to get the ink flowing. It may be that you have the opposite problem and your ink is flowing too fast and 'blobbing' on the page. Again, check your consistency and adjust accordingly. You may be loading too much ink onto your nib, so after you have dipped your nib, 'brush' off any excess on the edge of your ink container.

Ink bleeding

If your ink is bleeding, causing a feathery look to your letters, you may have a problem with the paper or the ink. As mentioned earlier, some papers work better than others. One tip to try when using glossy paper is to spray a fine layer of hairspray onto it before writing. If the ink is bleeding, you can try leaving the lid off overnight to thicken it.

Letterforms

Sometimes you may feel your letters just do not look right. Remember that perfecting letterforms takes time, patience and practice. It can be a very small tweak or change that can make all the difference. If your letterforms still aren't working, go back to the alphabet section and remind yourself of how they should look.

kisses ♡ hugs ♥ kisses ♡ hugs ♥ kisses
hugs ♥ kisses ♡ hugs ♥ kisses
happy birthday
happy birthday
happy birthday
happy birthday

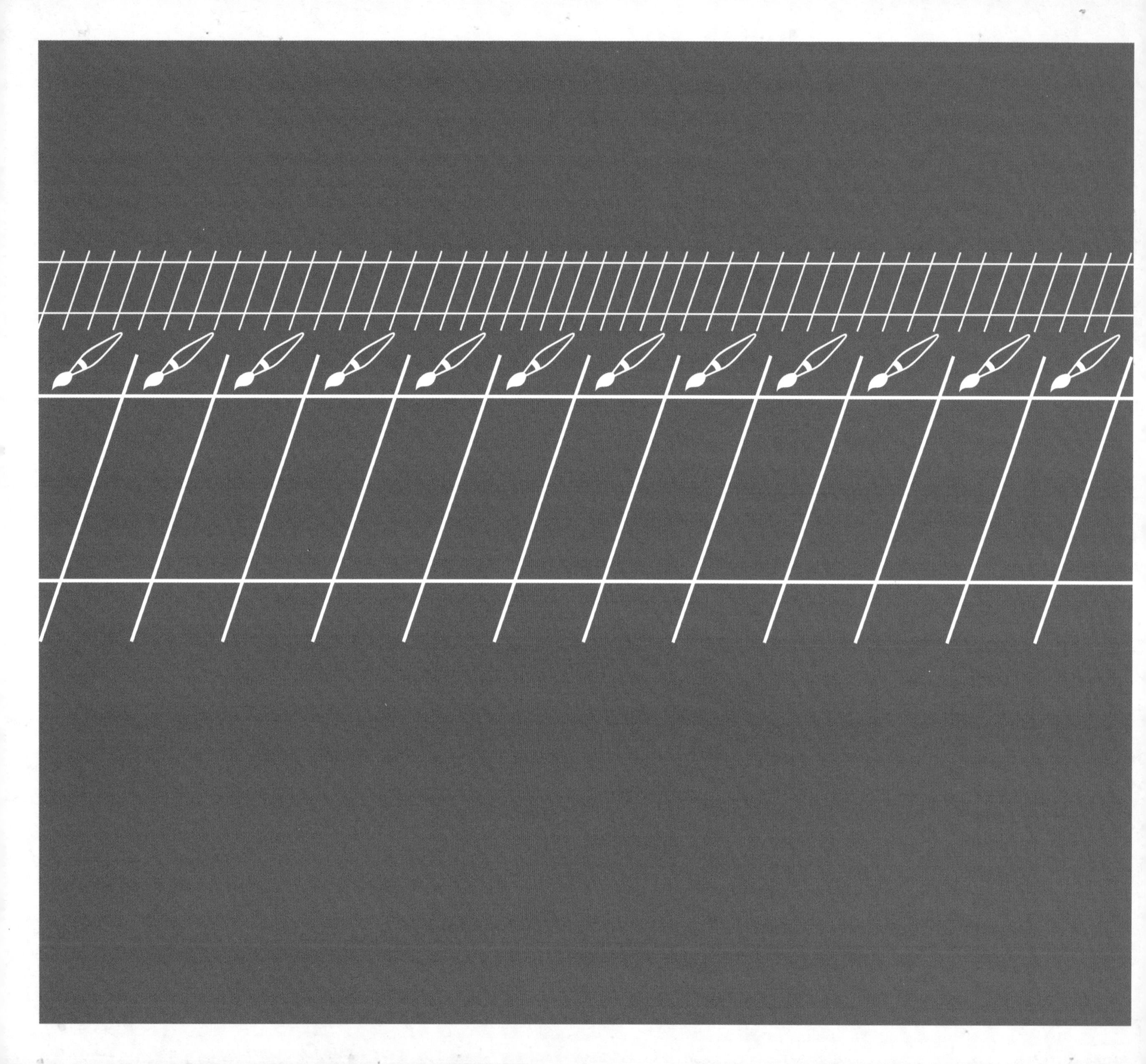

BRUSH LETTERING

Style

Contents

About the artist

For me, making signs started before brush lettering. I liked using words to make art rather than imagery, and these took the form of hanging and standing signs. I tried techniques such as screen printing, vinyl and woodcutting while I was at art school and, while I loved the results they produced, there was a lack of immediacy to them—you had to prepare a screen or wait for the vinyl to be delivered. What I wanted was the freedom to come into the studio, put on my apron and just start painting in the manner that a traditional painter or artist did. This is why brush lettering appealed so much to me; you can just grab some paper, pick up some brushes and start painting.

When I started brush lettering, I lived above a pub and persuaded the manager to let me use an empty room upstairs to practise in. I had a blank piece of board, some paint and brushes, and I set about trying out some different styles I had seen. It was pretty bad lettering, but I was enjoying it. I studied styles of other letterers that I admired and built a collection of alphabet and signwriting books that I flicked through. Most of the styles I practised and still use today are classical shapes, but I always try to put in my own little flourishes here and there—something that I think really makes the lettering 'pop'.

I started wandering into pubs and other businesses, asking if they needed a signwriter. I would spend my days off in my studio making artwork that incorporated signwriting, and whenever anyone's birthday came around, they would be extremely unsurprised to receive a hand-lettered sign, saw, box, or whatever I could find in the local junk shops.

I founded Irregular Signs to give myself an identity as a signwriter. The name is a reflection of the kind of work I want to produce—something a bit different. I draw a lot of influence from the tradition of signwriting that has preceded me, and when I say something a little different, I don't necessarily mean something that hasn't been done before, but instead something different from what I see day to day. Consequently, I often find myself striving towards the aesthetics of older lettering styles, and I am forever trying to pick up new techniques.

I work out and about in London, signwriting on fascias and windows for bars and restaurants, painting posh numbers for houses in Mayfair and lettering on street-food trucks. I also work from my studio in Streatham Hill, creating everything from quick paper sign commissions to 20-foot shop fascias, designed, painted and ready to be delivered and fitted. I like to do a couple of sessions every week, practising my lettering styles and researching new techniques so that my skills continue to evolve. I see my work in equal parts both a romantic pursuit and a practical job, and I want it to stay that way!

Archie Salandin
www.irregularsigns.com

Brush
IRREGULAR
SIGNS
WWW.IRREGULARSIGNS.com

About brush lettering

Brush lettering is infectious. Once you get an interest and start creating your own lettering and signs, you suddenly observe a whole world you walk past every day and didn't know existed. You start to notice words that you have seen and obeyed or ignored, and see them in a whole new way. It's an odd pastime; it will spread to your friends and family, and before you know it you will find yourself being sent pictures of old signs your friends saw on holiday. Your photo library will be a series of unconnected words and styles writing a nonsensical poem for you to flick back through. You cannot pick up a pen without doodling the strokes of a new style you are interested in.

Until relatively recently, brush lettering (in the form of signwriting) was one of the only ways to have a business branded. There has, however, been a shift away from hiring signwriters. Now a shop owner can order printed vinyl lettering or banners to adorn their shop fronts, or pick from the many pre-set fonts that come with a word-processing package. It is therefore easy to generate a sign quickly without having to consult a specialist. In other words, signwriting is no longer a necessity, but instead one of the many options for people when they need signs or lettering.

Having said that, there is always a very worthwhile and valuable place for brush lettering. Aside from it being more durable than printed letters, it also has a certain 'bounce' that printed letters cannot replicate. That is not to say that it is wonky or rough, just that it subtly shows the touch of a human hand. Signwriting now walks a thin line between practical craft and art form. People hire signwriters because they want the individuality of painting by hand, not just because they want a sign.

The distinctiveness of hand-painted signs comes from the particular lettering and sign composition that a competent signwriter can bring. Spending the time learning how to draw letters so that you know exactly how you want them to look is an essential skill in brush lettering. If you have these letterforms embedded in your mind, then you know how they work together, which styles complement each other, and whether they will suit the context in which you are painting them. When you become accustomed to how you want your styles to look, you can stop sketching out fully formed drawings of the letters, and instead make simple impressions to guide you, using your muscle memory of the brush strokes needed to form letter shapes.

You will often find that lettering in your workshop is very different from painting on site. There are always extra complications, such as a rough surface to paint on, poor access, or a difficult client! It is worth taking the time to refine your letterforms so that you have one element that you know is under control. You will find that each job requires a unique approach, so it's good to have a number of different alphabets and layouts in your toolbox, allowing you to adapt to any situation in which you find yourself.

There are also many different reasons why signwriters are favoured over other methods. Some people have house numbers and honours boards painted because it fits with a tradition that has been passed down throughout the years. Tattoo parlours have their shop fronts lettered by a professional because they trade in creative designs and quality of craft, and a cheap plastic sign would send out the wrong message. Small businesses often support other small businesses and won't necessarily have a graphic design or marketing department like many larger brands, and therefore they appreciate the input of a specialist.

The next sections will give you an insight into techniques that are essential for traditional signwriting and developing your own brush lettering style.

Materials

Over time, you may collect hundreds of different tools and brushes. Some will be useful and others you will probably never use after the first time. It's always fun to have new toys, but it's also a good idea to get acquainted with your basic toolkit. This can be divided into four categories: stationery, brushes, paints and tools.

STATIONERY

Pencils, ruler and compass: These are your basic drawing-out tools. HB pencils tend to do the trick.

Stabilo pencils: These are 'grease' pencils designed to write on any surface. They are handy when you are painting on glass or a painted surface, as you can remove the marks with a damp rag. They come in many colours, but white and yellow are the easiest to remove.

Charcoal and chalk: These also offer great ways of marking out, and can be wiped away afterwards.

BRUSHES

There are millions of brushes that are used for signwriting, with different lengths, hairs and shapes. The three listed below are the most commonly used.

Sable hair chisel: This is your 'go-to' brush for painting most letters, as it gives you the freedom to pallet it more or less (see pages 102–3). The end of the brush comes to a nice chisel shape so that you can get sharp corners, and you can also change the width of your brush stroke, making it a nice versatile brush for most of your needs. If you're going to buy one brush to get started, buy a number 5 sable chisel. This gives you all you need to get practising.

Sable or synthetic flat: This brush is great for block lettering, It has a permanent sharp corner and easily maintains a uniform stroke width. I tend to use this type of brush mainly for larger block lettering.

Sable pointed: This brush comes to a point at the end rather than a chisel, so it is great for doing fancy script-work that has plenty of thicks and thins.

PAINTS

I tend to use One Shot Signwriting Enamel and Poster Paints for most of my brush lettering. They are oil-based so they don't wrinkle paper, and they flow really well. The Signwriting Enamel is very high gloss, making it durable for exterior use. The Poster Paint is matt and faster-drying, making it ideal for practice and poster painting (obviously). You can thin these with white spirit or odourless thinners to make them less viscous.

TOOLS

Lolly sticks and disposable shot glasses: You can pick these up from most poundshops or household goods stores, and they are great for stirring and mixing paint.

Palette and dippers: My preferred way of painting is to put a shot glass in one dipper (a small pot that clips onto the side of a palette) and some thinner in the other—this way you have your own little workstation that you can hold in one hand.

Mahl stick: This is a tool that some lettering artists use to steady their hand (see also page 102).

Good ways to practise

I find the trick with practising is to never make it seem like a chore. When I am trying out a new lettering style, I will usually spend a lot of time repetitively sketching it out, over and over, while I'm listening to the radio or sitting on a train. Memorising shapes by drawing them out will make things so much easier when it comes to painting, and integrating this practice into your daily routine will really speed up the process.

I practise painting on cheap paper or glass. Glass is more difficult than painting on wood or paper; there is less friction, so you have to think very carefully about your brush strokes. This might seem frustrating at first, however, when it comes to lettering on a sign, it means you will be much more confident in your technique.

It's important to practise your brush lettering in a fun way as well as productively. Painting an alphabet over and over without anything to use it for is rather unsatisfying. If you want a quick finished piece, you could paint a showcard, that is, a sign painted using poster paints on a piece of card. It's as simple as that! Otherwise, try painting up some wood and make your own sign, or find an unusual surface to paint on.

COFFEE
WHISKEY

Basics of painting

HOLDING THE BRUSH AND PAINT

There are three main ways to hold your brush and paint, to make it as easy as possible to do your lettering.

mahl

1. The first method is to hold the pallet in your left hand (assuming you are right-handed) with your paint pot attached, while also gripping a **mahl stick** with your left hand. A mahl stick is essentially a stick that rests on the surface you are painting on, with some cloth wrapped around one end to prevent it from marking the surface. It gives your painting hand something to rest on so that you have space to make longer brush strokes without resting your hand on potentially wet lettering that you have already painted. This method looks the most complicated, but it also gives you a lot of freedom to make long, loose brush strokes.

2. The **hand over** method involves resting your painting hand over your non-painting hand. Again, the purpose of this is to allow your painting hand to have space to work while still being steady enough to paint straight lines.

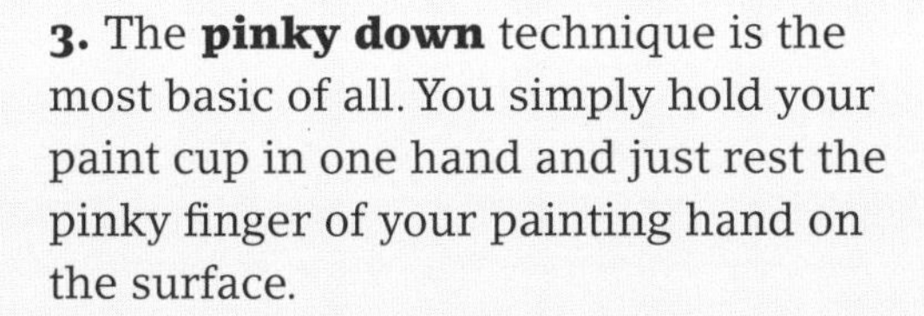

3. The **pinky down** technique is the most basic of all. You simply hold your paint cup in one hand and just rest the pinky finger of your painting hand on the surface.

In order to paint long, even strokes, you need to load up your brush with paint correctly. This is something that will require a lot of trial and error.

You need to dip your brush in the paint and then flatten it out a few times on either your pallet or the rim of your paint cup (depending on whether you use a pallet or not). The purpose of this is to spread the paint evenly onto your brush and to make sure there is not too much paint on it so that it doesn't drip.

If you are using a chisel brush, the secondary purpose of this flattening process is to create the shape you want. To make greatest number of strokes, you need to flatten it out fully and paint with the whole brush on the surface. This gives you a nice sharp chisel shape. However, you can also pallet it less if you want to obtain a thinner stroke, painting with the tip of your brush only—for instance when you are painting the connections of script letters.

Measuring the letters

Before you start drawing out words, here are a few tips:

Always draw a top and bottom line: Even if you are using a really casual style and intend to go up and down and all over the place, it's helpful to have an intention of where you want your lettering to be. It will only take a second more to draw those lines.

Centring: Unless you are intentionally aligning your lettering left or right, you need to centre it. A good way to achieve this is by 'scratching' it out first. This means roughly pencilling in the letters with single strokes to gauge how close to the centre to start your lettering. If this is not correct, rub the letters out and pencil them in again (see illustration right). It also helps to mark out a centre line first.

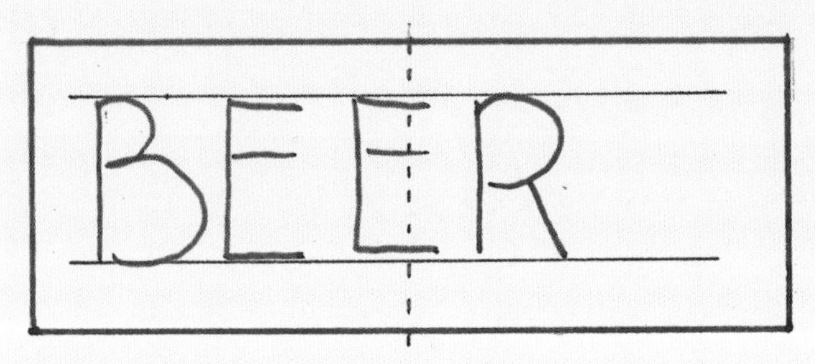

Initial scratch out—not centred

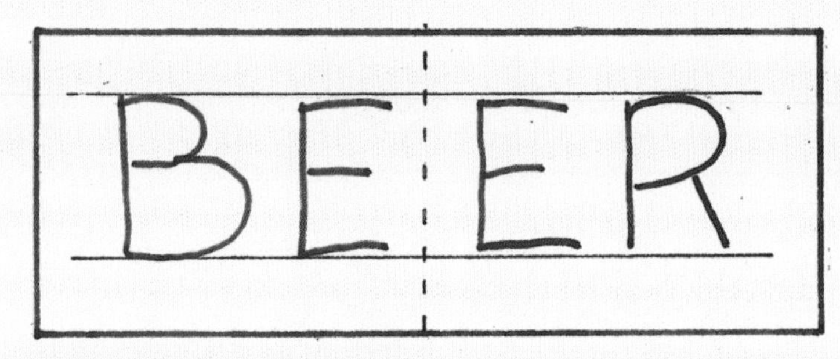

Corrected scratch out—centred

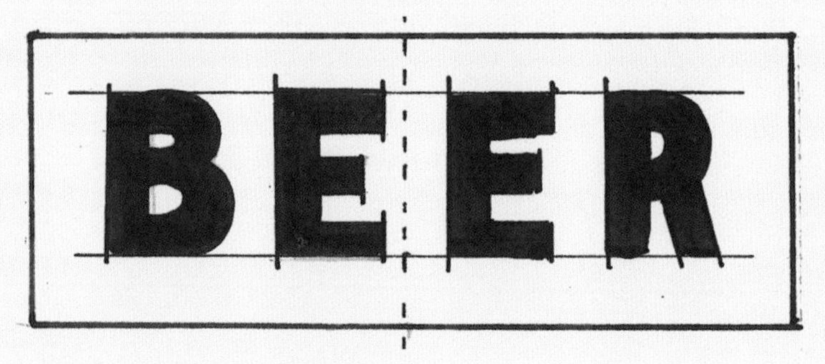

Drawn out and painted letters

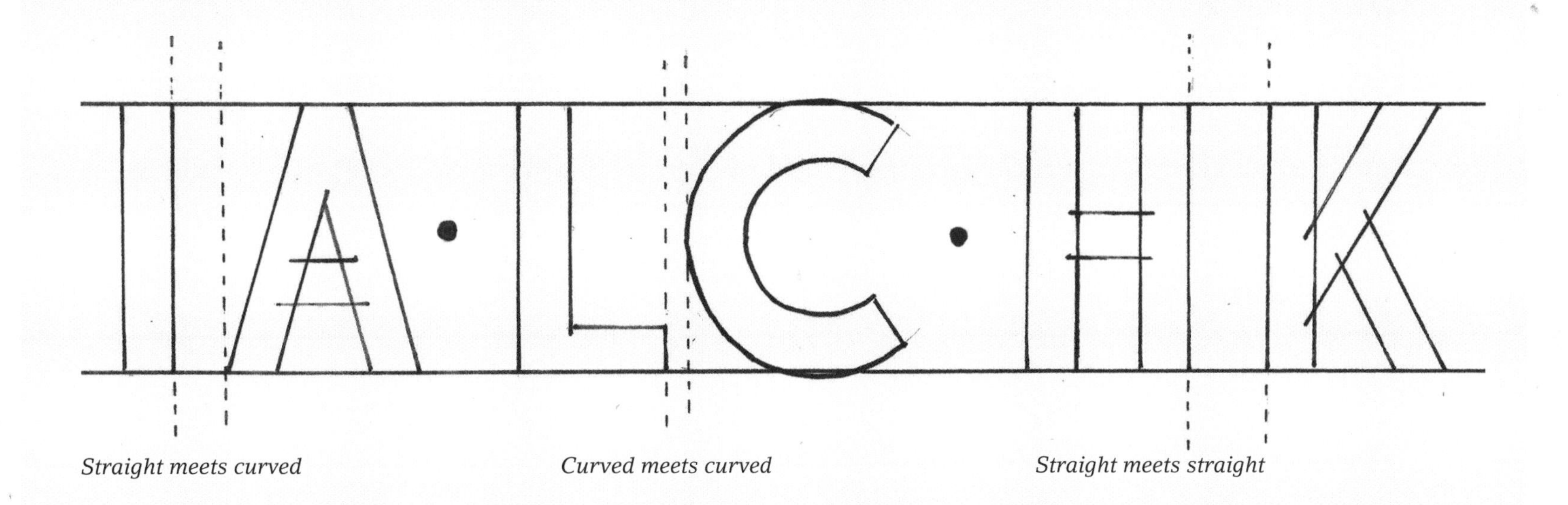

Straight meets curved *Curved meets curved* *Straight meets straight*

Think about your spacing: When placing letters next to each other in a word, it is important to think about the space between each letter. This is known as 'negative space'.

A straight side meeting a curved side needs more space between the letters than a curved side meeting another curved side. Conversely, a straight side meeting another straight side needs even more space than that (see illustration above).

In this context, a curved side is any side that is not a straight vertical, for instance the right-hand side of an 'L' and either side of an 'A' is considered a curved side as much as either side of a 'C' would be.

Lettering STYLES

Lettering styles

There are many wonderful styles of brush lettering to try out. Here, we explore some of the most important ones to add to your repertoire: block lettering, script, traditional script, Roman, casual, Victorian Fairground, Art Deco, angular and shaped writing, 3D letters and shadows, and prismatic effect. After mastering the basics, it's fun to experiment with variations and flourishes.

Block lettering

Block is one of the most important lettering styles for a signwriter and definitely the first to get practising. It is simple and eloquent but has so much potential for personalizing, making it a great alphabet to have in your box of tricks.

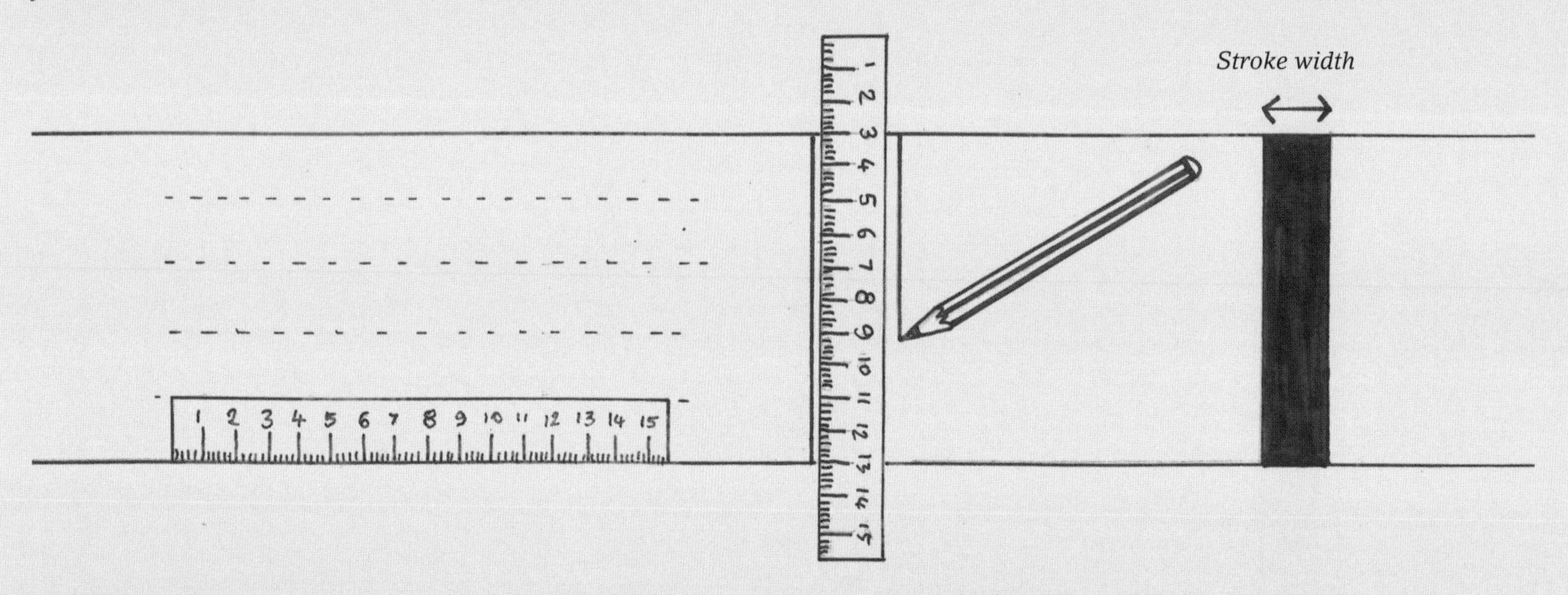

Composing your lettering

This lettering style is constructed from blocks of uniform stroke width with no serifs, which keeps things simple when drawing it out. My top tip for drawing block is to use the width of a ruler as the stroke width. I measure the height of the lettering as five or more times the width of the ruler, depending on how compressed I want the lettering to be (see also page 112). I tend to carry lots of different-sized rulers in my toolbox so I can quickly sketch out any size of lettering.

The first step is to draw out your top and bottom lines. In the example above, I have used a letter height that is five times the stroke width. This gives you a nice chunky block letter.

You can use a ruler as a guide to make measurements, but don't be afraid to ignore it. The best rule is: if it looks right, it is right.

Things to note

Where there are curves, I have drawn guidelines to keep a uniform width and maintain symmetry. Where possible, especially if you are executing large lettering, it is best to use a compass to draw these curves. Note that curved letters also sit slightly above the top line and slightly below the bottom line.

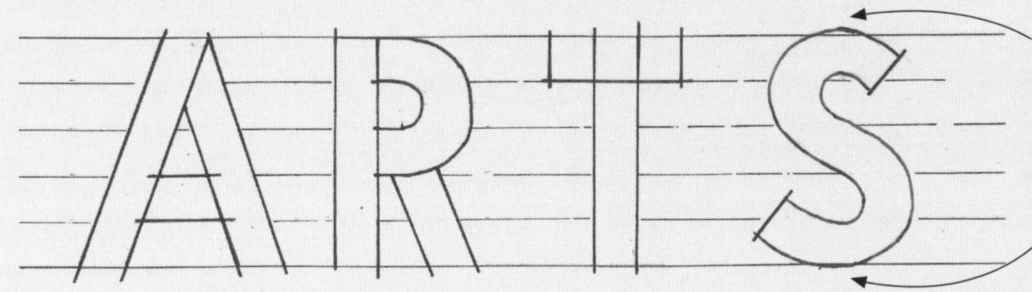

When drawing an 'S', it is important to make sure the top is smaller than the bottom; this is also true of the letter 'B'. This rule is echoed in almost all lettering styles.

When painting this block style, there are a few basic moves that you need to practise:

Vertical stroke: This is always done from top to bottom, twisting the brush at the bottom of the stroke so that it tapers into a point (see Step 1). To make this stroke into a block, a second short horizontal stroke that also tapers is then made to turn this stroke into a rectangle (see Step 2). The angled and horizontal blocks are also made using this method.

Painting a curve: This is always painted from top to bottom, but can be clockwise or anti-clockwise. When painting a curve, you need to twist the brush as you go around the curve so that it maintains the same width all the way around. I find this is made easier by holding the brush between your thumb and first finger only.

These building blocks allow you to construct any letter you need, and after much practice you will be able to paint block letters with only a scratch outline.

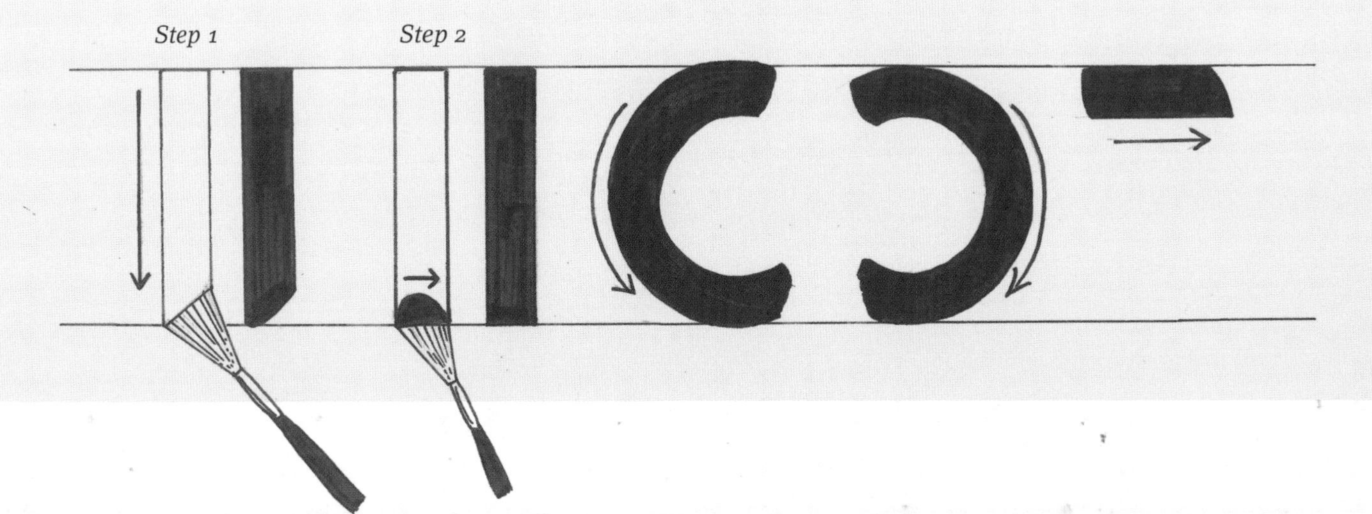

Block alphabet

Here is an example of the full block alphabet sketched out, with construction lines included so you can see the steps you need to take to draw each letter.

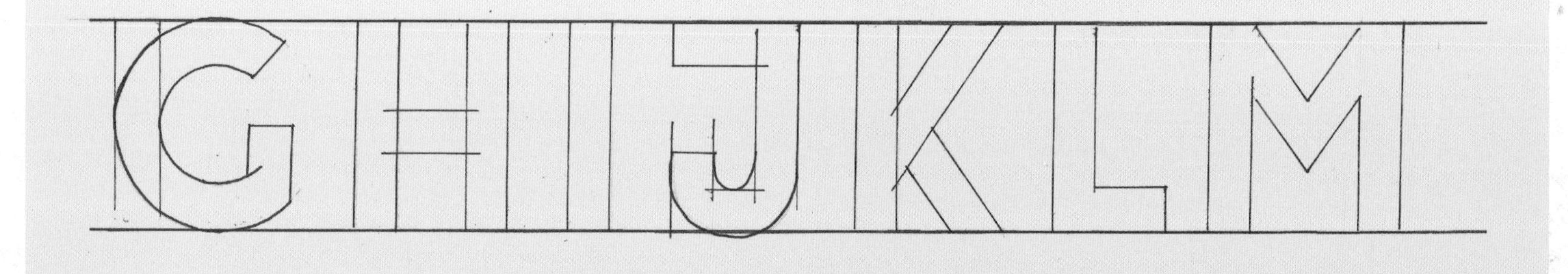

NOPQRST
UVWXYZ

Accents, special characters and variations

Here are some examples of ways to use accents, special characters and variations in your block lettering.

You can use a standard size of accent, or you can use a stylised large one like the example shown on the second 'E' below. Many smaller flourishes can be made on individual letters, mainly by altering the horizontal strokes of letters. Some examples are shown here.

Have fun and experiment with your lettering, but always make sure to keep it legible!

Once you have got used to lettering block, you can try out some variations. Try increasing the letter height but keep the stroke width the same. The example here (top right, where you can see an alternative way of drawing out the 'O' and 'C' letters that are normally quite wide) uses a height of seven stroke widths, and the result is a compressed letterform, which is useful when you want to fit lots of text into a small space. Note how the curves flatten out at this height.

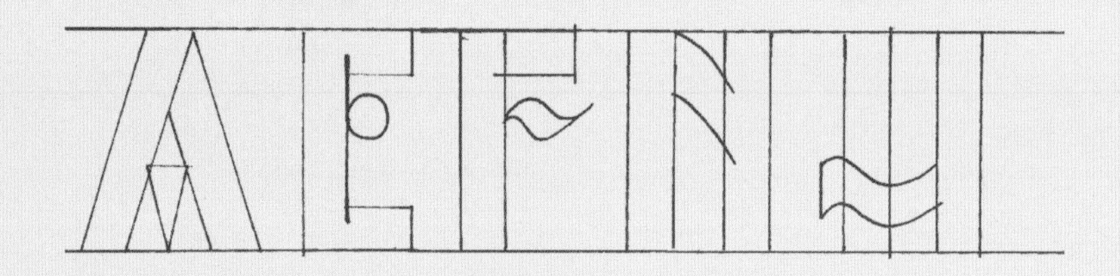

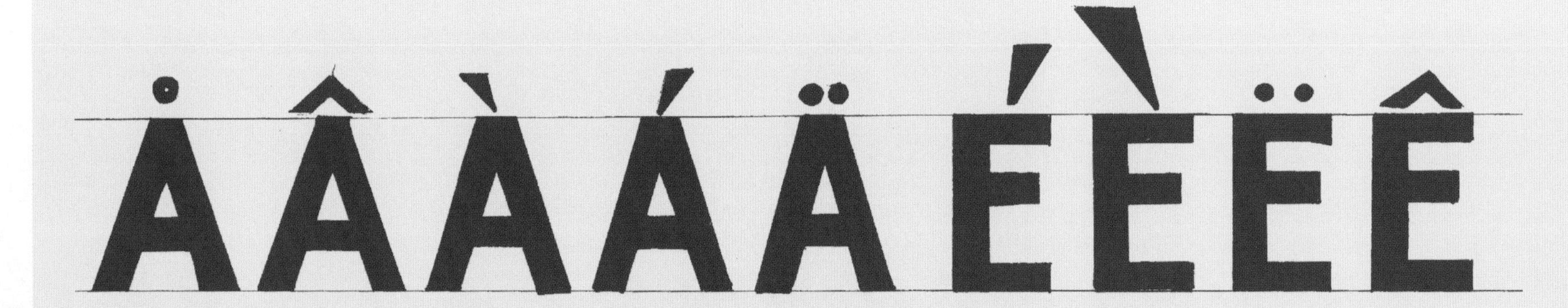

Ø Ö Ô Ò Ó Õ Ç Æ

. , : ; ~ ’ “ ” ! ? & £ € $

Script

This is a nice loose style that has so much room for personalisation. Every lettering artist develops their own style over time. Once you've established this, you'll have a great style 'signature' to put into your work.

Script letters are made up of a few single strokes joined together by thin connecting strokes. The basic move is a thick downward stroke that turns into a thin upward stroke at the bottom. This is achieved by paletting your brush to a wide chisel when beginning the stroke, twisting the brush at the bottom to get a smooth transition, and then lifting it off as you make the upward stroke, thus decreasing the thickness of stroke as you pull the upward stroke. It is worth practising this stroke many times over before starting to put whole words together.

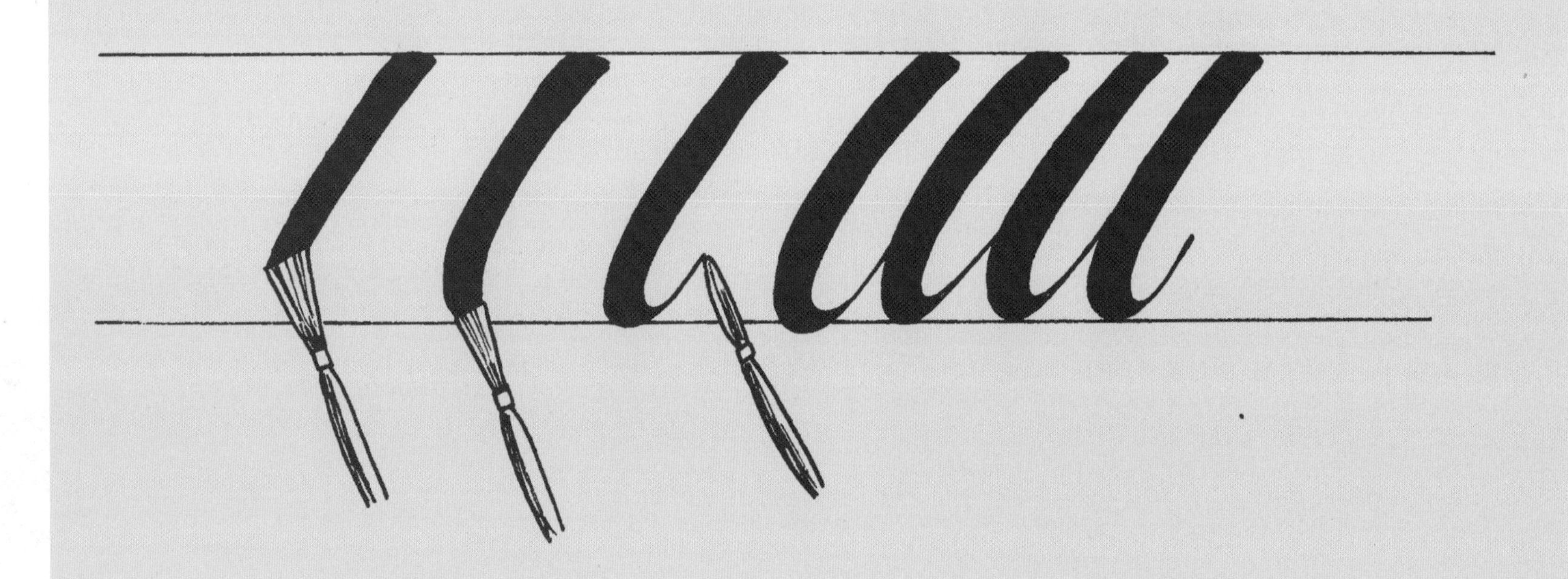

The script style is best executed by making a quick layout, then moving straight to painting, as it is the shape of the brush strokes that really defines the lettering. The key in making a good script is consistency. This style can be executed upright or at a slant; either way, you need to maintain a consistent angle throughout. A good way to practise is to draw out parallel lines before lettering, and then using these as guides for the angle of your brush strokes. Notice that the downward strokes of curved letters such as 'e' and 'c' have a greater angle than those of 'I' or 't' (see pages 116–19).

When practising, try to paint out whole words rather than an alphabet, as the joins between letters are different depending on which ones are connecting.

Script alphabet

Here is an example of a script alphabet. Most of these letters will join with each other, however, the occasional one—'b' for example—is best left unjoined.

lmnopqrstuv

wxyz

Script capitals

These tend to be slightly embellished adaptions of either lower case script letters or quite similar to casual letters (see pages 136–141). You will notice that some of these have places where they can join to the next letters and some don't. Don't feel like you need to join up the capitals; a lot of them will look good just as they are.

N O P Q R S T

U V W X Y Z

Accents, special characters and variations

Here are some of the accents and special characters that are useful for lettering in this style. Script is a style where you can really let loose with making variations. You can change the proportions of the thicks and thins, making a thick script, or you can keep the width the same throughout or make it heavy-bottomed. These have to be suited to the context in which you are painting, as they will work in some places but not in others.

Thick

Fat Script

Uniform

å â à á ä é è ë

ê ø ö ô ò ó õ ç æ

. , : ; ~ „ “ ” ! ? ¢ £ $ €

Traditional script

This is a classy, joined-up lettering style, often seen accompanying Roman lettering (see pages 130–35). It is more elegant than your signature script and requires a greater level of brush control. This style is best drawn out in full and then lettered with a pointed brush.

Strokes are made with thick going down, thin going up, and all lettering needs to be done at a slant. The five main strokes are shown below. Try to keep your curves smooth, and chisel off the tops of letters such as 'b' with an understated horizontal stroke.

You will find that by pulling the brush almost completely off the surface in the upward strokes, you get a very nice thin joining line. A good way to practise is to do a few sheets of joined-up 'A's before starting to paint other letters or whole words.

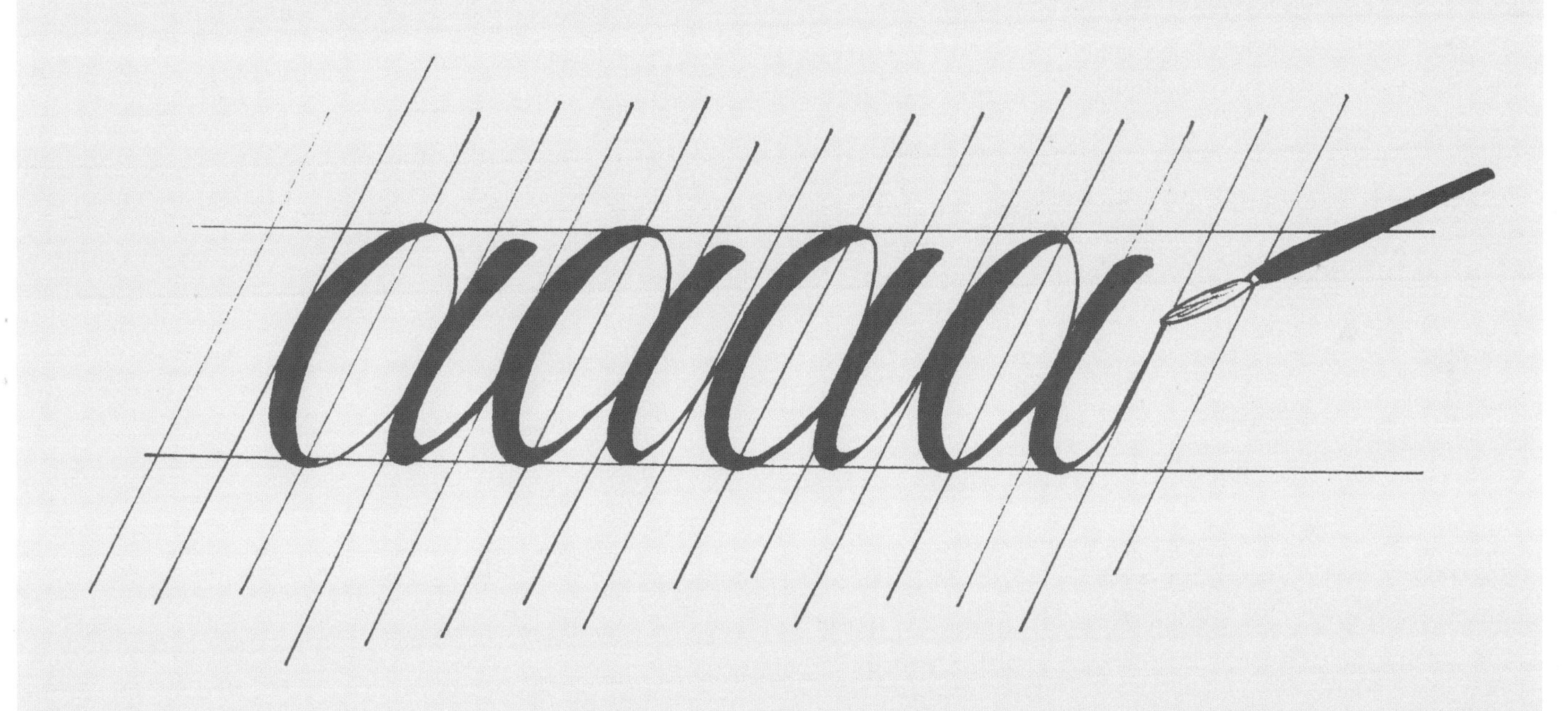

Traditional script alphabet

Here is an example of a full alphabet in the traditional script lettering style.

i j k l m n o

pqrstuv

wxyz

Traditional script capitals

This style is one with very ornate capitals. The letters themselves might not look very clear to read, but in the context of a whole word they easily make sense. Never do brush lettering using only capitals, as your writing will be illegible!

O P Q R S T

U V W X Y Z

Accents, special characters and flourishes

Here are some of the accents and special characters that are useful for the traditional script style.

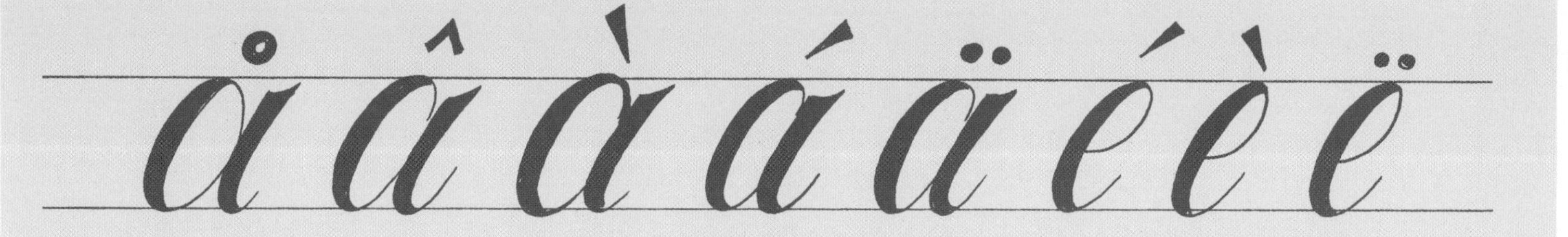

ê ø ö ô ò ó õ ç æ

Flourishes in traditional script are delicate. There's a risk of going overboard with long, swirling flourishes, so remember that the more of them you add, the less legible they are. Think about the context in which you are executing this type of brush lettering—it might be great for a logo, but bad for lettering that is trying to convey information.

Roman

This is the most widely used alphabet in the world. It is a traditional style designed to be lettered by brush, as its thicks and thins and the weighting of its curves make it easy to paint with strokes from a brush. Unlike any of the other styles in this section, it has 'serifs'. These are the flicks at the tops and bottoms of the letters.

The Roman letter is made up of two different stroke widths, one twice as thick as the other. The basic letter 'I' is made up of two strokes: using a chiselled brush, you start with the tip of the brush and flick to the right, then bring it down in a thick stroke that you taper off and flick to the left. You then execute a mirror image of the same stroke,

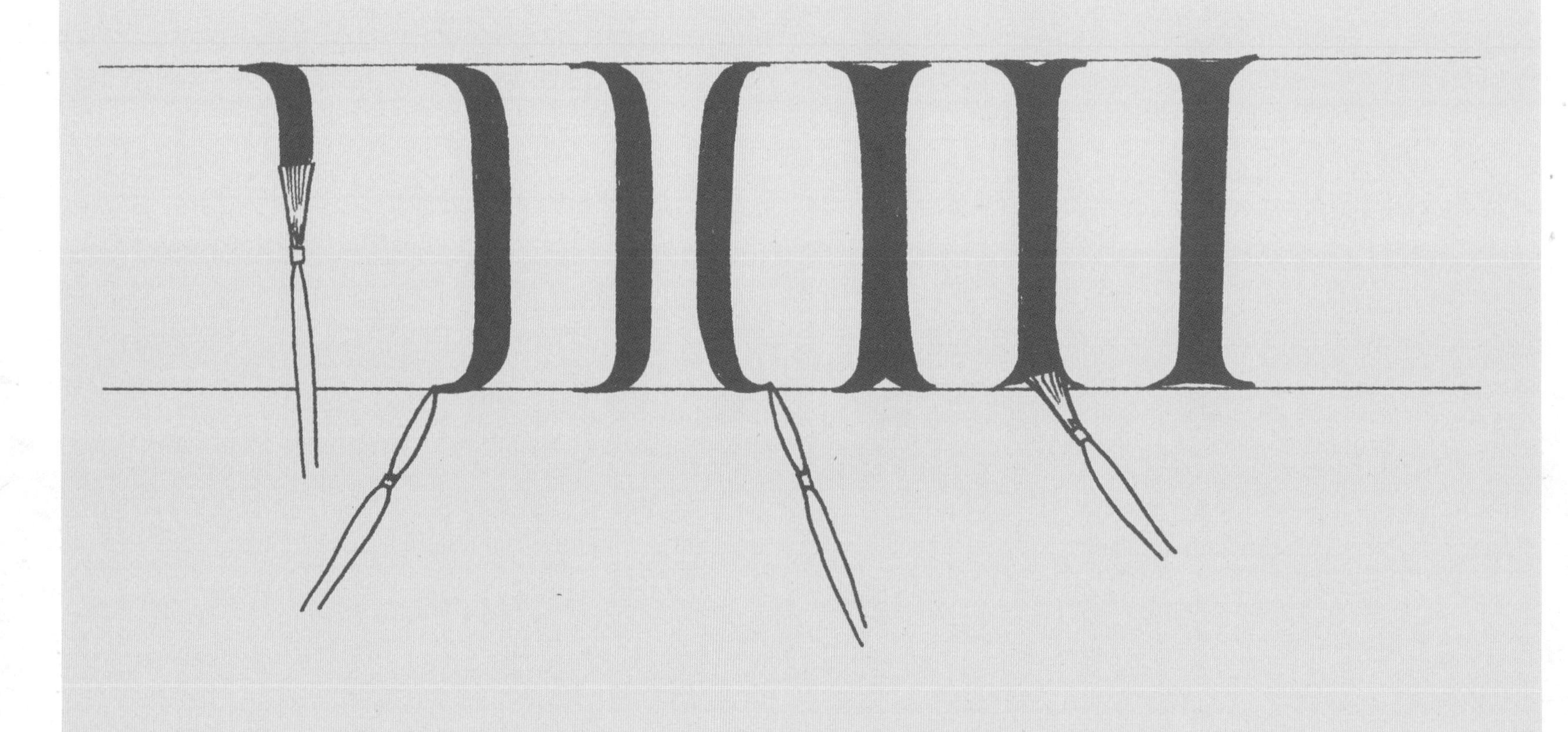

the thick of which occupies the same space as the first stroke. This can be cleaned up at the bottom with a short horizontal stroke. All horizontal strokes are thin, and the curved strokes go from thin to thick and then back to thin again. Curved letters such as 'O' have the weight of the curve positioned so that the thicks are at the 2 o'clock and 8 o'clock position. The 'S' is composed of a central stroke starting thin and ending thin, then two square serifs are added afterwards.

This style will take time to get used to drawing out and painting. It's actually quite quick to master once you get the hang of it, but like all styles, practice is the key to success.

Roman alphabet

Here is a full Roman alphabet drawn out.

A B C D E F

G H I J K L M

NOPQRS

TUVWXYZ

Accents, special characters and flourishes

Roman lettering accents should always be understated, because it is an elegant alphabet.

ËÊØÖÔÒ

Ó Õ Ç Æ &

. , : ; ~ ' ' " " ! ? £ € $

You should always err on the side of caution when adding flourishes to Roman lettering. Unlike script or casual, adding too many flourishes will disrupt this style. Below are a couple of examples that you can try out. When painting on a sign, I would only use one of these (choose which letter will look the best).

Another good variation of this style is to exclude the serifs from the alphabet.

EA

AE

MEN'S

Casual

This type of lettering is a style you will see more in the United States, however, with the resurgence of signwriting it has migrated over to Europe and many other parts of the world. It is a fast lettering style that is very useful for showcards and small type, but can also be executed to make slick headers for your signs.

Casual is quick to draw out, fast to paint and can be refined to make your own unique signature style. It is most commonly seen at a slant, but can also be done as an upright. As usual, draw a top and bottom line and scratch out the words you are writing. If you are drawing out the slanted version, then draw yourself some slanted parallel lines to guide your angles.

One reason the casual alphabet can be drawn rapidly is because it is made up of just a few different strokes. Unlike the script style, there are no thin strokes and you execute almost all the letters in a downwards or left-to-right direction (for a right-handed painter).

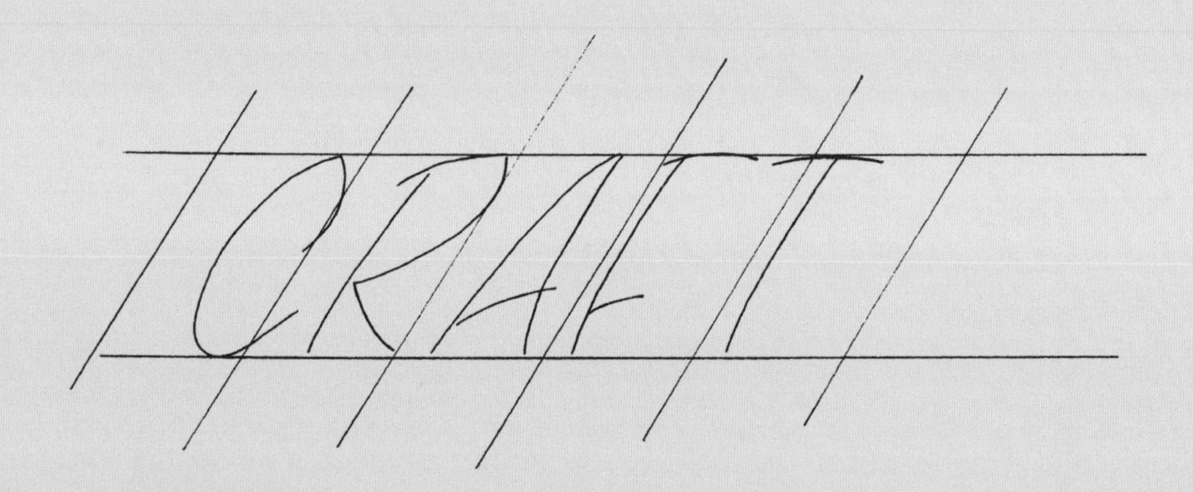

The fine detail that makes a good casual alphabet is in the tops and bottoms of the strokes. Unlike block lettering, you don't do a horizontal stroke to square off the tops and bottoms, and you don't join up your letters like in script. The bottoms of the strokes are rounded off with a little twist of the brush, giving you a neat swash shape.

This can be exaggerated or understated to make different variations. The letters also have a certain 'swing' to them—they are not quite straight but very slightly curved strokes. Mastering the fine detail of casual lettering is something that comes with repetitive practising and gauging how curved to go.

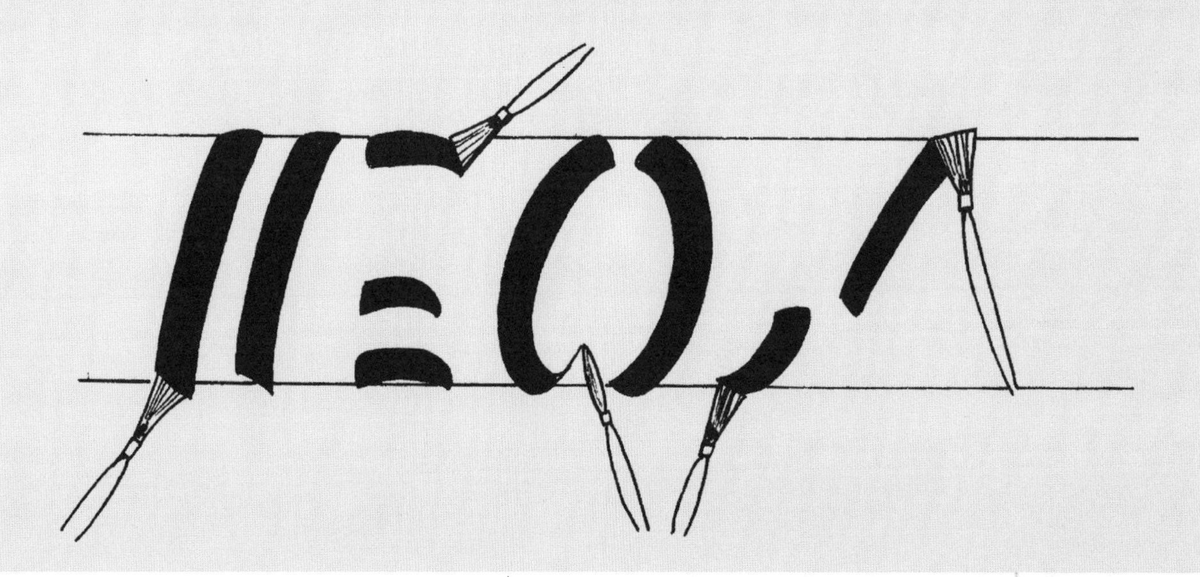

Casual alphabet

Here is a simple example of a casual alphabet.

ABCDEFGH

IJKLMNO

PQRSTUV

WXYZ

Accents, special characters and variations

Here are some of the accents and special characters that are useful for this casual style of lettering.

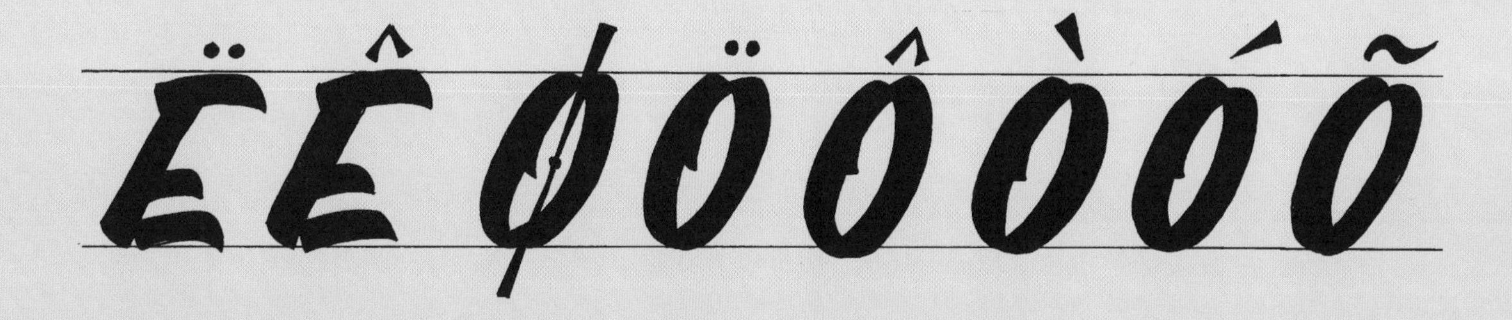

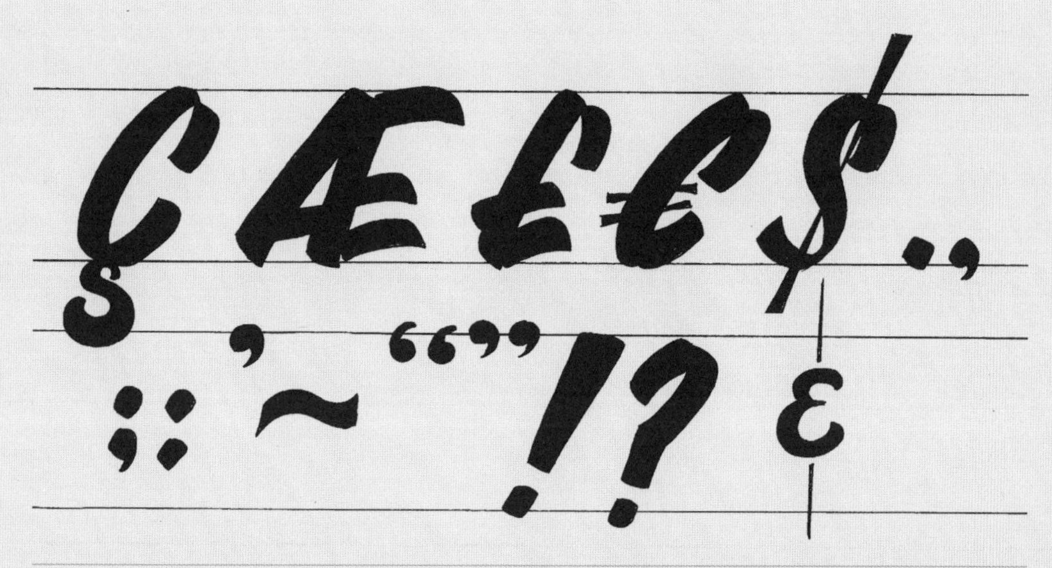

Casual has a lot of opportunity for variation. Altering the thickness of the strokes, changing the sharpness at the end of the strokes and changing the angle at which you slant them will give you a plethora of different results.

While it is necessary to have the basic strokes and casual alphabet ingrained in your mind, each individual combination of letters presents a chance to try out something new. Below are some examples of full words lettered in casual.

FRIED
WINGS

HOT DOGS

Victorian Fairground

This style is a kind of cross between thick and thin and Roman. It is a style that I would draw out without using a ruler, as it is the curved shapes of the letters that really give it its form.

You paint this alphabet in a similar way to Roman, but in place of the long serifs that characterise Roman, you have little spurs instead. When painting this style, I always make the bottom of the stroke slightly concave.

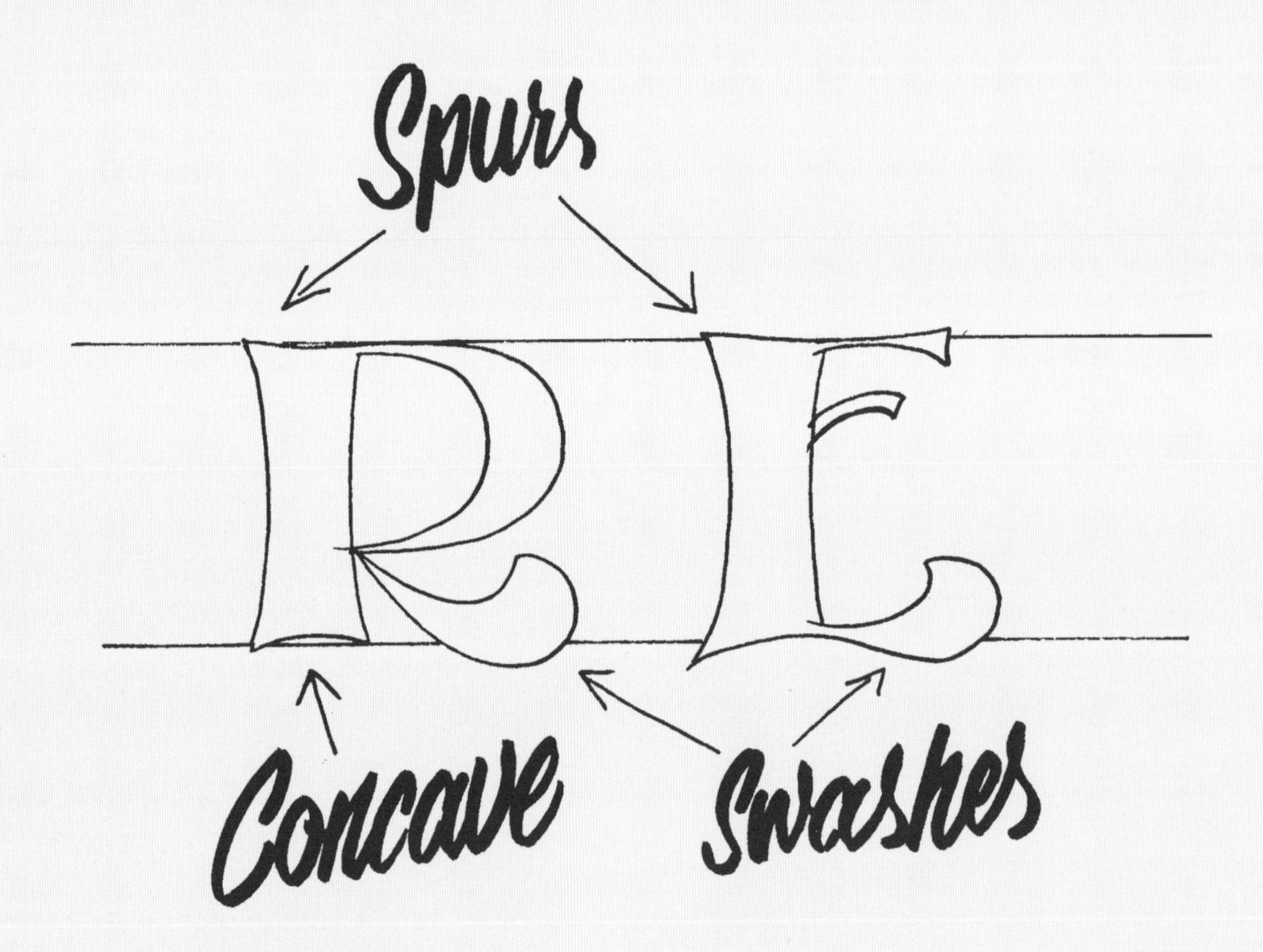

FINE
WINE

This is a style that has a lot of in-built flourishes. For instance, the right-hand foot of the 'R' (see opposite) and the bottom stroke of the 'E' have swashes. Try to keep these the same shape throughout, to keep the style coherent.

Victorian Fairground alphabet

Here is an example of a full alphabet in Victorian Fairground style.

ABCDEF

GHIJKLM

NOPQRS

TUVWXYZ

Accents, special characters and variations

It is fun to use the shape of the Victorian Fairground swash as an accent where you can, or else use big accents to mimic the letters.

È Ë Ê Ø Ö Ô Ò

Ó Õ Ç Æ . , : ; ~ „ “ ”

! ? & £ $ €

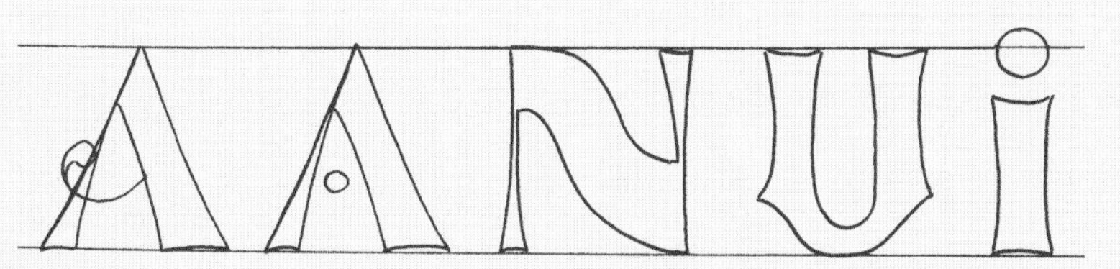

With this style, it is best not to add in too many more variations than are already included. To the left are some minor adjustments you can make to refine your style. I usually stick to one version of each letter within a context.

Art Deco

This style is particularly popular in gin bars and other trendy establishments. It is quite quirky and won't fit in everywhere, but looks great when used in the right context.

It is based on the thicks and thins of Roman lettering, but exaggerated to the extreme. The thicks are many times thicker than the thins, and on curved letters there is an instant switch from thin to thick.

The Art Deco alphabet can be sketched out and painted very easily. To aid drawing, use a ruler of the same thickness you want your thicks to be, then roughly mark in the thins. You can use the width of your brush stroke to paint the thins in one motion, then fill in the thicks with a few strokes.

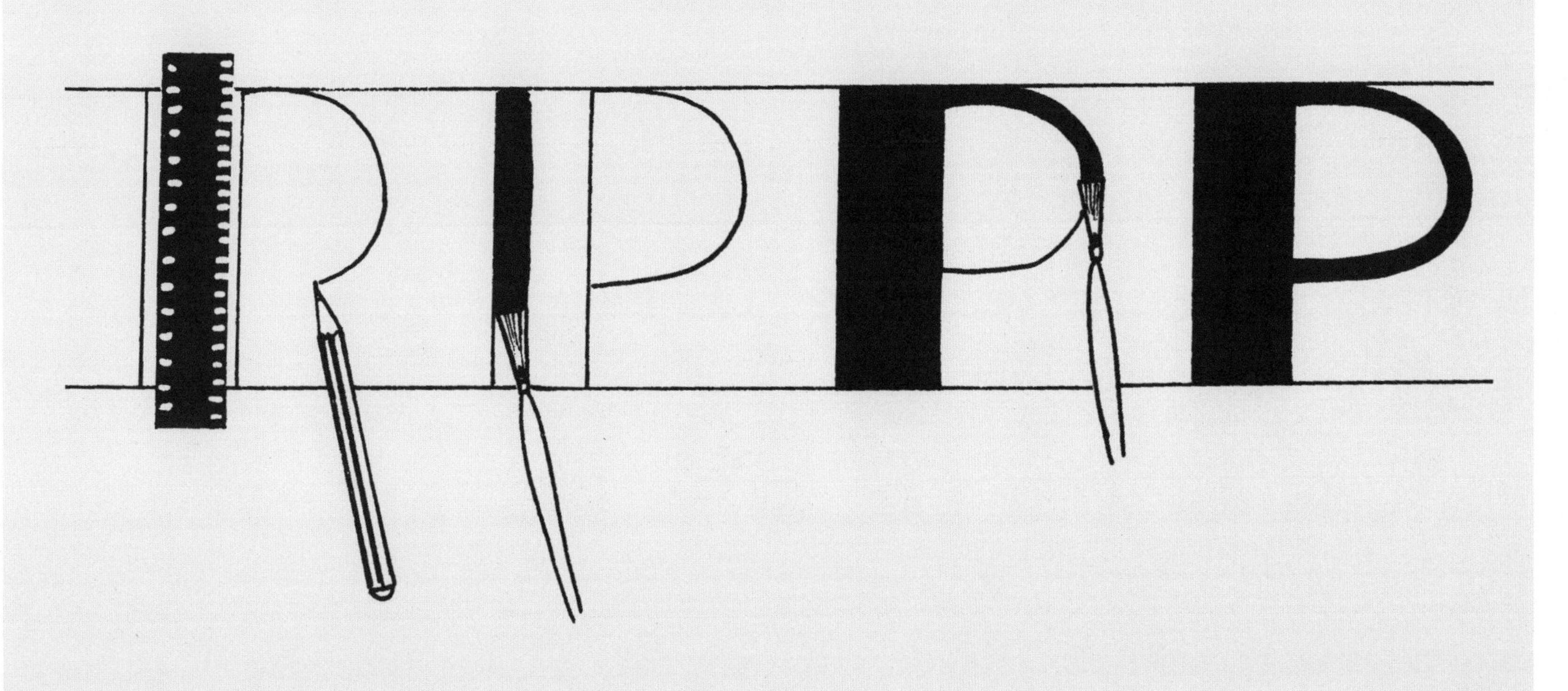

Art Deco alphabet

Here is an example of an Art Deco alphabet.

ABCDEF

GHIJKLM

NOPQRS

TUVWXYZ

Accents, special characters and variations

You can be bold with your accents and special characters in the Art Deco lettering style. It's a very showy kind of alphabet, and benefits from being flamboyant.

ÈËÊØÖÔÒ

!?&£$€

Changing the height of Art Deco lettering gives you quite a few different variations for this style. Try making it many times higher than the examples on the previous pages. You can also try adding spurs to the letters to make them less rigid. With this style, it is the subtle changes that will make your lettering stand out.

TEA TEA

TEA

Angular and shaped writing

One way to make brush lettering more interesting is to paint it at an angle or have it wrap around a shape. However, bear in mind that not all lettering styles will look good when shaped.

Script and casual tend to look good at an angle, especially when they lean towards the angle. Block letters tend to work well when put on a curve, whereas letters with serifs and more free-form styles such as casual do not.

It is worth weighing up how much you want to play with the shape of the letters against any flourishes you have put into the letters. Simpler letterforms will be more effective if they are wrapped around a shape.

EVENTS

JOIN US FOR

3D letters and shadows

There are many effects that you can add to your lettering to make it seem as though it is three-dimensional. Here are examples of the most common effects.

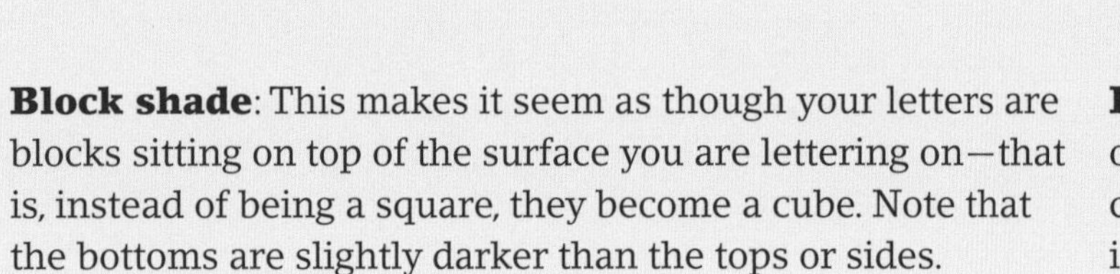

Block shade: This makes it seem as though your letters are blocks sitting on top of the surface you are lettering on—that is, instead of being a square, they become a cube. Note that the bottoms are slightly darker than the tops or sides.

Block with a shadow: This is a more convincing version of the block shade. By adding a shadow of a slightly darker colour than the background, it appears as if your 3D letter is casting a shadow.

Floating letter: By painting the same letter shapes slightly below and to the left (or right depending on your preference) in a darker shade of the background colour, it appears as if the letters are floating on top of the surface.

Quick shade: This is a quick way of producing a rough shadow effect. It is almost the same as the block shade, but there is a small gap between the letter and the shade. This can usually be executed without drawing out, and it has the advantage that you don't have to wait for the lettering to dry before applying it.

Prismatic effect

This is a technique of shading within the letters to create an illusion of them being three-dimensional. The principle is that it appears as though the letters stick out of the surface or are carved into it. It is achieved by using contrasting colours for the top right and bottom left segments of the letters, as if light is hitting the 3D letters and creating shadows.

The best way to work out which colour goes where is to think of the light being in the top right-hand corner of your sign and shining down onto each letter. If you want it to appear as if the letter is sticking out of the sign, make the top right area brighter than the bottom left. If you want it to appear as if the letter is carved into the sign, then do the opposite.

For a more detailed effect, use a four-colour system. The tops should be the lightest, followed by the right-hand areas, then the left-hand areas, then the bottoms.

numbers

123456789

Numbers

This section is separate from lettering style because it's rare that you'll use both numbers and letters in the same context. Numbers don't necessarily follow the same rules as lettering, and thus can be altered to suit your needs. As you will use them less frequently than letters, it's worth taking some time to practise exclusively drawing numbers to keep your skills sharp.

Block numbers

These follow most of the same principles as block letters. They keep a uniform width and have sharp corners and flat bottoms.

5 6 7

8 9 0

Roman numbers

These have many variations. They mostly get painted as house numbers, and therefore have no other context around them to match. Having said that, it is worth looking down the street in case there is a prevailing style that could be fitted into. This is an example of understated Roman numbers.

1 2 3 4

5 6 7

8 9 0

Casual numbers

These are great for prices and opening times. Like casual lettering, they are painted with single strokes and are a great way of working quickly.

5678

90

Layout ideas and combining lettering styles

When you start lettering, the urge is to combine every different lettering style you know in every different colour with all the different effects. Fight that urge! Try just using two or at most three different styles in each sign, and pick ones that contrast, such as script and block, or Roman and traditional script.

GATSBY

GIN~WINE~BEER

the
BURGER
Mansion

What's most important? The first thing to think about when laying out a signs is: what is the message you are trying to convey? If it is a food and drink offer, then the price is usually the most important item, so pick a bold style that will jump out to the viewer. The next most important information would be: what is the offer? Finally, the details of the offer are painted in smaller type. A quick layout for a price-offer showcard is shown here. A block and casual style is used mostly for impact, with the smaller writing being in script for speed. This sign has three styles on it, but would work just as effectively if 'BEER' was in the same block style as 'BURGER'.

Margins and decoration: Leave large margins in your work—there is no point in crowding the whole surface with lettering, as it will only become illegible. Having a good balance of lettering and negative space will make your sign the most readable.

A little decoration goes a long way. Adding a simple border or one quick effect to the text will make it appear more like a finished piece of work.

Tips

PRACTISE!!!!! I cannot stress this enough. Just sketch out some letters while you have the television on, or paint one alphabet every day. It won't take you long to see improvement.

While you may be eager to start painting, it is worth taking the time to **master the sketching stage**. This will make your life a lot easier when it comes to brush lettering.

You don't need to have a job as a signwriter to start lettering—just start painting letters and making signs. **If someone has a birthday coming up, paint them a sign!**

Build yourself a portfolio. Apart from making signs in your spare time, offer people you know your services in exchange for food or beer. We have all done it—it's a nice way to paint jobs that exist outside your house/studio, and free stuff is always nice for your friends to receive!

Don't be afraid to say that something is a bad idea. If your client is asking you to letter in a way that you think won't look good, then offer them an alternative. If they are set on it, so be it, however, there is nothing worse than executing someone else's poor design and then being criticised for how it looks after you have painted it.

Be a master craftsman. You will find yourself much more satisfied with your work if you do things properly. Whether it's rubbing out all the layout you just sketched because it wasn't quite centred, or painting a second coat on the white lettering because it didn't cover very well (this will happen), it is 100% worth the extra time. Take pride in your work.

Have fun. Lettering is the best job in the world, so make sure you enjoy it!

The End

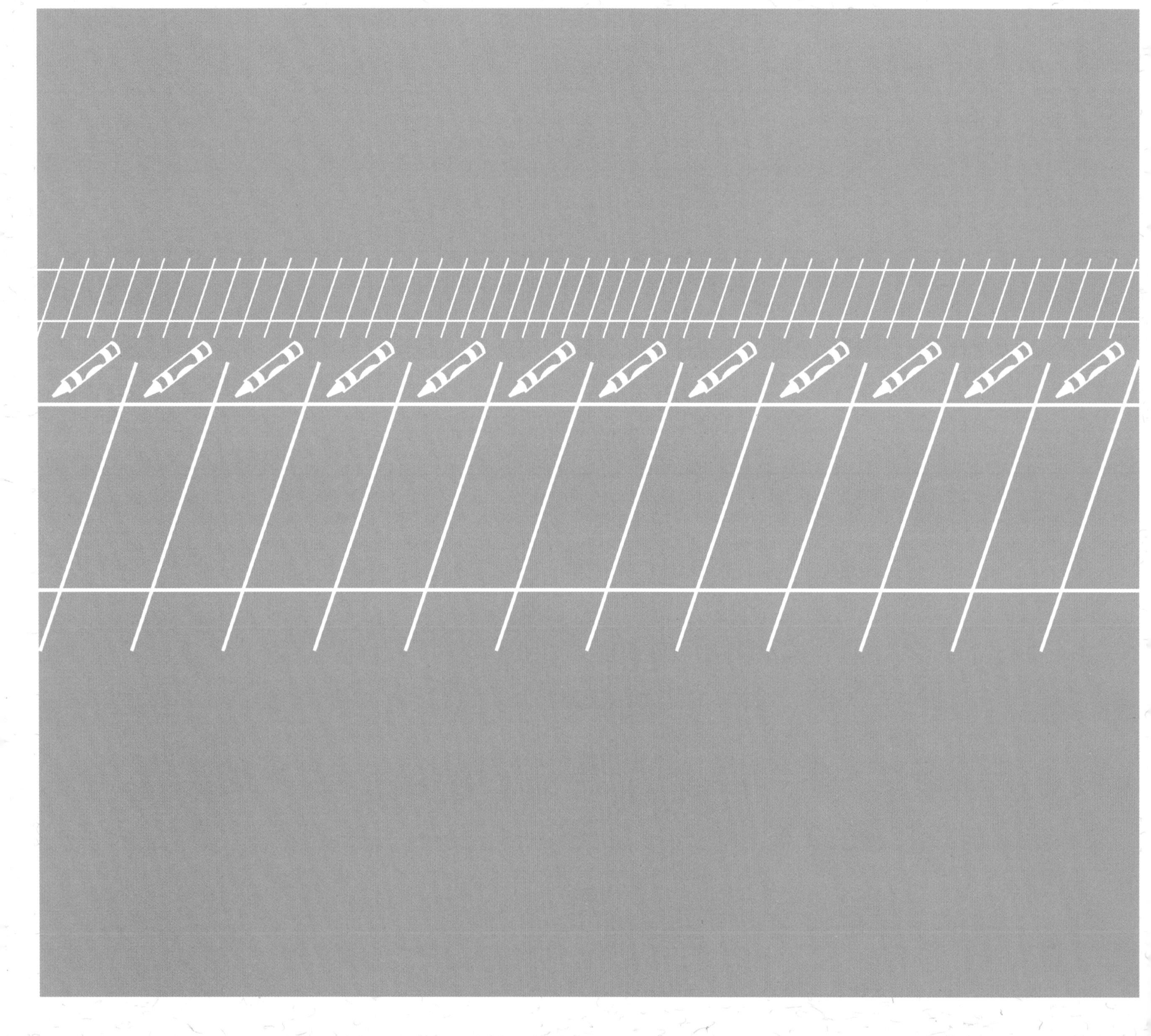

BLACKBOARD LETTER ART

€$&!?.,

Pp Qq

Contents

About the artist

I've always been a very creative person. From a young age, cult films and posters, album artwork, urban clothing brands and street art have heavily influenced me. I've always had a natural habit of picking up a pencil, pen or paintbrush and expressing my creativity on a blank canvas. Either drawing from my own imagination or copying an object right in front of me, I've always had a passion for art.

I pursued my interest in art by completing an Art Foundation Diploma at UCA Epsom, where my love of hand lettering really began. I would always try and incorporate type and hand lettering into my artwork, trying different techniques and taking inspiration from the typography used from propaganda posters.

The more my interest grew in hand lettering, the more I began to see hand-painted work all around me. One day in particular, I was sitting in a pub and noticed how perfectly all the blackboards were signpainted, each letter was painted with accuracy and precision. I really appreciated the skill that had gone into the boards, so I spoke to the barman about who had painted the boards, and he told me that a sign-writer comes in to do all the work in the pub. It was from this point that I began my journey into the trade.

Since that day, I have worked hard to make being a blackboard artist my full time job. I began by doing blackboards in my spare time when I worked in hospitality. It was exhausting, but my passion to keep the trade and skill of hand lettering going strong kept me motivated. Eventually I made the leap to being self-employed and starting my blackboard business full time.

I feel very lucky to have a job that I love, where every day is different. I get to work in different parts of London and meet different types of people and it feels great to know that I am helping businesses improve their ability to connect with their customers through my artwork. I love that I carry my 'workshop' with me in my rucksack to each job I do and I feel a great sense of freedom and creative control. Through my work, I have developed a strong understanding of branding and how to communicate a business's message, which also drives me to be more inventive each time I paint a blackboard.

My business, The Blackboard Artist, is continuing to grow, to the point where I now custom-make boards and have a great team of skilled sign-writers working with me. I am excited to keep developing and growing my passion, I hope to share my knowledge through this book and inspire you to also work on your creativity with hand lettering.

Michael Tilley – The Blackboard Artist
Instagram: @theblackboardartist

THE
BLACKBOARD
ARTIST

About blackboard letter art

Blackboard art is popular because it's bespoke and it's human. When I am doing a job, I find that people are always curious about how I produce the work, and they enjoy watching it being created. Hand-painted lettering illustrates the artist's character and people appreciate that human connection. I feel it's important to keep hand-made crafts alive because using your creativity to produce something using only your skill and passion is so rewarding.

Traditional skills, trades and crafts are definitely making a comeback. Much of society is saturated with technology, impersonal communication and mass marketing. People are starting to make a conscious shift to spend their money in smaller independent businesses, helping skilled artists and craftspeople to earn a living. Signwriting is a part of this shift in culture, as more people admire the skill and personal touch that hand lettering can bring. The skill is more than just making something look attractive, it's about identifying the theme of a business so that the blackboard can build on the branding, helping to promote a product or service more effectively.

Previously blackboards were more commonly associated with pubs, but nowadays they are used absolutely everywhere: from weddings and events to street food stalls and classy bars. Blackboards can also be used at home to write down daily tasks, or even in a child's bedroom providing a space to go wild with creativity using chalk. It provides a nice smooth surface to work on and it has a great rustic look to it. Hospitality remains one of the most popular sectors to find blackboard art. Today, restaurants and bars have to pay more attention to the lettering they use to represent their brand. These independent businesses require something unique and bespoke to suit the products and services they are providing.

One of the benefits of having blackboard art rather than printed design is that it can be amended or regularly altered. If you print something and you're not happy with it, you're stuck with it. With blackboard art, if it needs to be changed, it's just a simple case of painting it out and redoing the signage. Boards can change all year round with celebrations like Easter and Christmas, or simply to promote a new product or midweek deal to grab a customer's attention when walking past.

Businesses know that people recognise and appreciate the skill that has gone into creating good blackboard art and this makes it an important form of marketing. However, blackboard art doesn't have to be just for advertising. If you want to improve your illustration and lettering skills, and just let your creativity flow, I would really encourage you to get a blackboard and start experimenting.

Materials

For painting lettering onto your blackboard, you will need to buy the following materials online or in your local art shop:

- A small tin of Rustins quick dry blackboard paint.
- A medium-size paintbrush, or a small roller and tray.
- A small spirit level, to make sure your lines are straight.
- A metal ruler 30cm in length, for measuring.
- A Swan Stabilo Chinagraph All Surface Pencil in white.
- A black Molotow 227HS 4mm Round Tip Acrylic Marker (optional).
- A pencil sharpener.
- Some Molotow acrylic paint pens in white. I always use Molotow because the paint is strong and the nibs of the pens are really durable, but you can also use Posca and other acrylic paint pens for blackboards. You will need to buy five different sizes to outline your letters neatly and fill them in: 127HS Xfine; 127HS 2mm Round Tip; 227HS 4mm Round Tip; 4–8mm Chisel Tip; and the 627HS 15mm Broad Tip. These are all Molotow.
- A black pen (optional), to make your letters look a bit cleaner when you've finished. If you want to try some different colours, you can experiment with a broad range of interesting tones.
- A flannel or a J-cloth, to clean off pencil marks once the paint on your blackboard is dry.

Rustins
Black
ONE4ALL
ONE4ALL
ONE4ALL
STAINLESS

Making your blackboard

First of all, you need to buy yourself a small blackboard, or alternatively you can pick up a piece of medium-density fibreboard (MDF) wood. All the materials you will need to make your blackboard can either be bought online, from a timber merchant or from a hardware store.

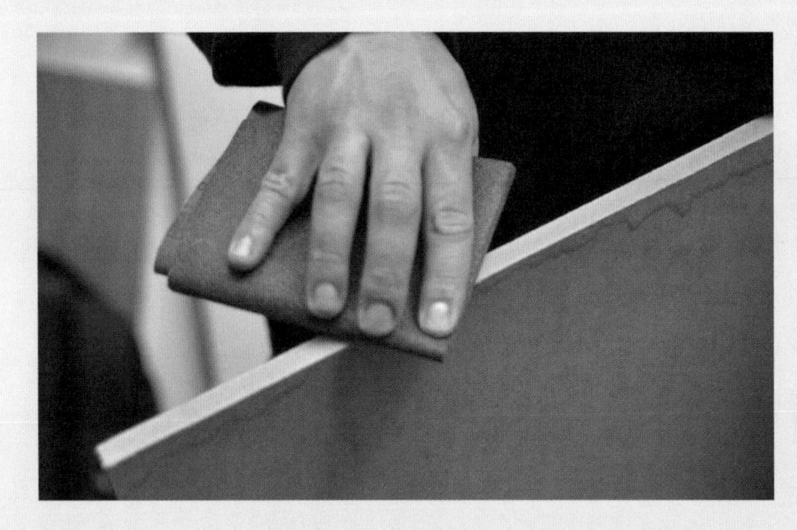

▲ First, you will need a some sandpaper to prepare the edges of the board. Sand the edges of the wood to ensure they are really smooth.

▲ Next, you will need a tin of Rustins quick dry blackboard paint and a medium-size paintbrush, or a small roller and a tray for pouring your paint into. You should work on a hard surface such as a table or against a wall. You might wish to cover it with old newspaper, as it can get a bit messy!

▲ Dip your paintbrush into the tin, then put an ample amount of blackboard paint onto the board. Spread it evenly so there are no lumps. If you're using a roller, pour some paint into your tray and use the roller to do the same procedure that you would with a brush.

▲ Continue painting until the board is completely covered with black paint. Once you've applied your first coat, you can use a hairdryer if you don't want to wait for the paint to dry. Make sure your hairdryer is a good 10cm away from the board, as the paint can bubble if you're too close to it.

▶ When your first coat is fully dry, apply another coat to the board using the same process. Paint the edges of the board too, and it's best to paint the reverse of the blackboard as well, so you have two sides to work on!

Measuring and marking up your blackboard

When your blackboard is completely dry and you are ready to begin, you need to plan where all the words and numbers are going to be positioned. When planning and marking up measurements, make sure your blackboard is resting on a solid, even surface—it can be either horizontally flat on a table or standing up vertically against a wall.

Use a spirit level ruler to make sure everything is level and accurate. If you have a few rows of text, you'll want to give yourself a little bit of space in between each row so that the text has a little room to breathe when you paint the letters onto the board.

Always pencil in your wording before painting. Having a rough guide for your lettering will really help you to spread the words evenly across the board. You can make the lettering more accurate when you start painting.

▶ Start by measuring the length and width of your board, making a note of your measurements as you go. Use a Stabilo Chinagraph All Surface white pencil and a spirit level to mark your horizontal and vertical rules. Next, find the midpoint by dividing the width measurement in half and marking it with your white pencil.

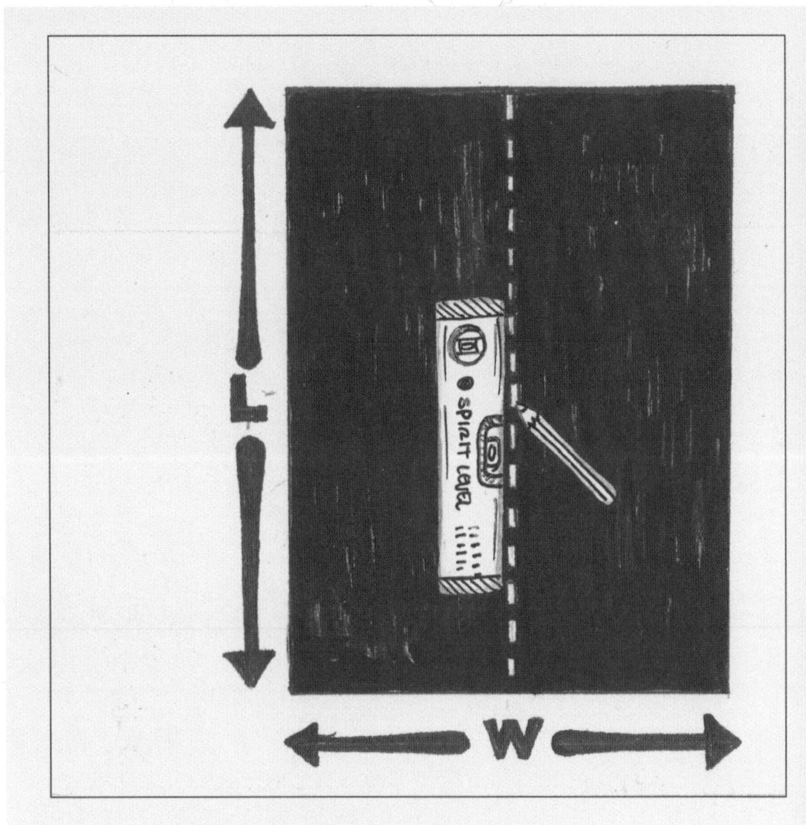

▲ Once you have the midpoint, continue to use the spirit level and white pencil to mark out a straight line down the middle of the board. Depending on how big your board is, make sure there is enough negative space from the edges of the board to where your letters will start.

▲ Taking into account the particular description or brief you are following, use the length to divide the board by however many lines you need. If you want to centralize your design, then the midpoint will come in very handy!

▶ Following the description you have, mark out the letters so that you have a rough idea where all your elements will be painted.

Example: Coffee & croissant

This is a good example to work from, and also a great way to practise creating your own script and block. These two letterforms are very commonly used to show a strong message, and are aesthetically pleasing to the eye.

In this very simple sign, the word 'croissant' is in a script style and the price is in a block style. It's a good idea to make the price big and bold, so that it grabs the reader's attention.

◀ First, measure and mark up where the words and numbers should be placed. Next, pencil in the description with your Stabilo white pencil.

▲ When you are happy with the position of your letters and numbers, mark over the pencil lines using a Molotow acrylic paint pen.

▶ When working on a script style like this, you need to give your letters a nice curve and a sharp finish. Make sure you connect them with a flow that leaves space between the letters as well.

◀ Fill in all the letters and numbers using a chisel tip, or if you're feeling brave enough, use a broad tip. When your piece is complete, study the letters you've painted and see where you can neaten up the edges with your 4mm, 2mm or Xfine pen. Choose whatever tip you feel most comfortable using. Once everything is tidy, you can then use a black Molotow pen to touch up any edges that may not be straight, or any paint spillage marks on the board, if you have any!

▶ You will then need to leave the paint to dry for a good 10 minutes. Once it's fully dry, dampen a clean cloth with water and remove all your pencil marks from the board.

Coffee

&

Croissant

£3.50

a Bb
d Ee
g Hh

T 8
8 A

TAXI

METRO

Different letterforms

In the pages that follow, I will be showing you a number of my own hand lettering styles that I have used for my work on a daily basis. Existing styles that I have endeavoured to make my own have inspired some of these letterforms, and I have created my own as well. There are blank lines under each alphabet for you to practise on. Study the letterforms carefully, but also be creative as you develop your own style with them.

Script

This is a popular and therapeutic style of lettering that I like to use for coffee shops and pubs. It's pleasing to the eye, and it's all about creating your own style and rhythm with it. Try your best to go thick with the stroke when you paint downwards, and thin when you paint upwards.

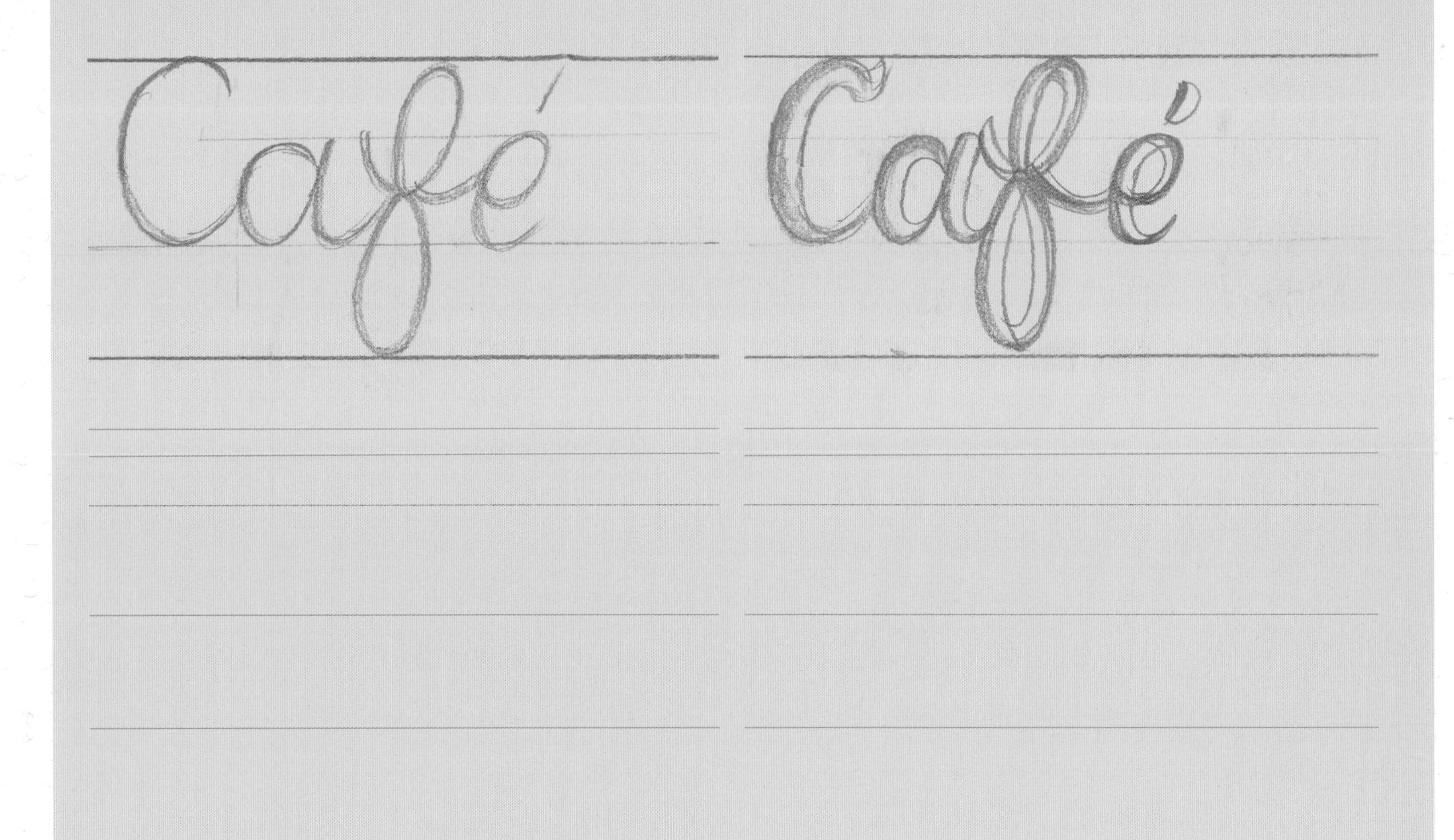

Café

Café

Script alphabet

Aa Bb Cc Dd Ee

Ff Gg Hh Ii Jj

Kk Ll Mm Nn Oo

Pp Qq Rr Ss Tt

Uu Vv Ww Xx Yy

Zz

Accents

å â à á ä é è ë ê ø ö

ø ö ô ò ó õ ç œ

Numbers and special characters

1 2 3 4 5 6 7 8 9 0

£ € $ & ! ? . , : ; ~ ’ ‘‘ ’’

Block

If you want to make a bold statement or promote a bargain price on your board, then block is the best way to do it. This is a strict letterform, and if you construct it well and take your time with it, you will be happy with the results.

Airport Airport

Block alphabet

Aa Bb Cc Dd Ee

Ff Gg Hh Ii Jj Kk

Ll Mm Nn Oo Pp

Qq Rr Ss Tt Uu

Vv Ww Xx Yy Zz

Accents

å â à á ä é è ë ê

ø ö ô ò ó õ ç œ

Numbers and special characters

1 2 3 4 5 6 7 8 9 0

£ € $ & ! ? . , : ; ~ ' ' ' " "

Rough bubble

I like to use rough bubble lettering for fun. You don't need to think too much when you paint this style. Give it that organic, hand-drawn feel, making sure it's really thick for maximum effect.

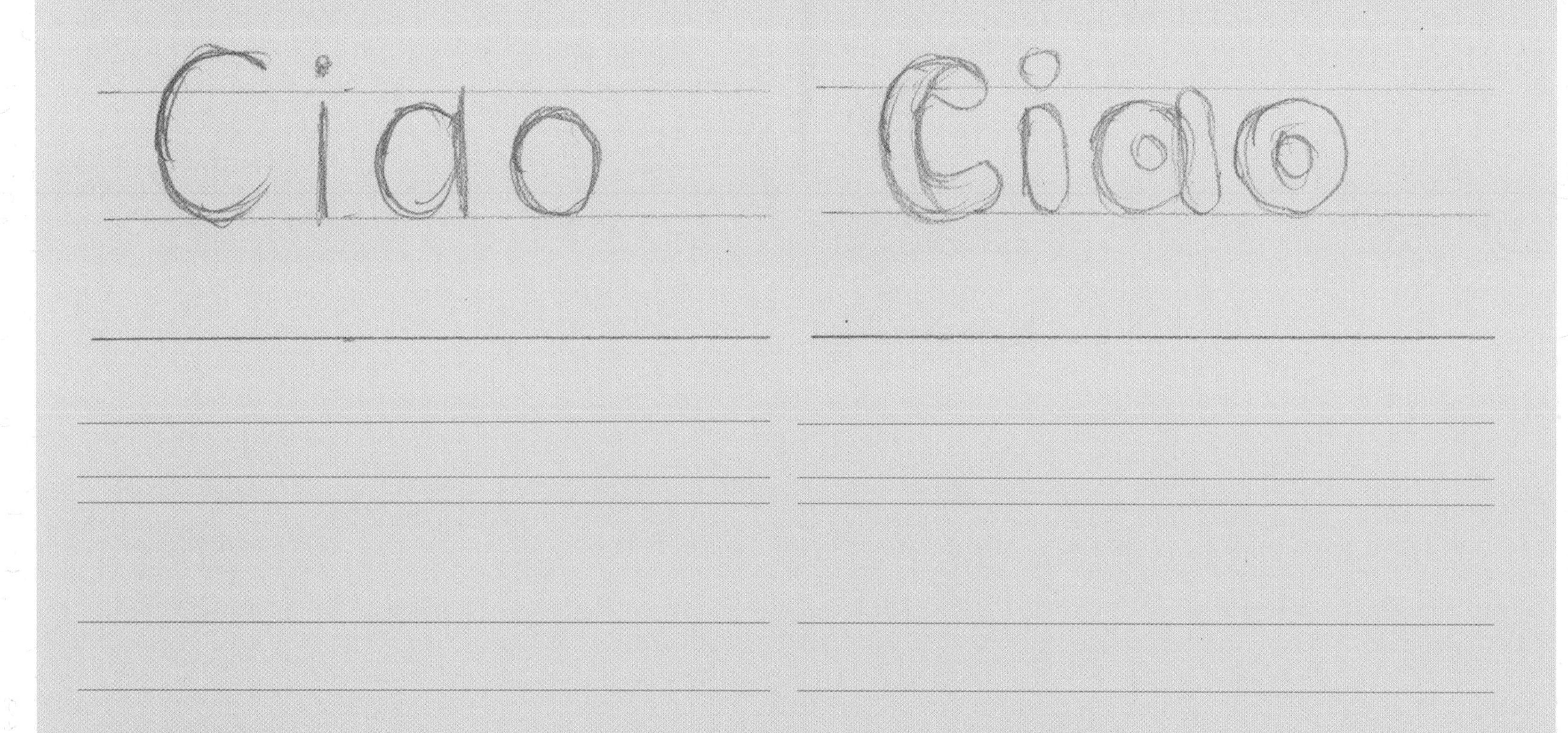

Ciao
Ciao

Rough bubble alphabet

Aa Bb Cc Dd Ee

Ff Gg Hh Ii Jj

Kk Ll Mm Nn Oo

Pp Qq Rr Ss Tt

Yy Zz

Accents

å â à á ä é è ë ê

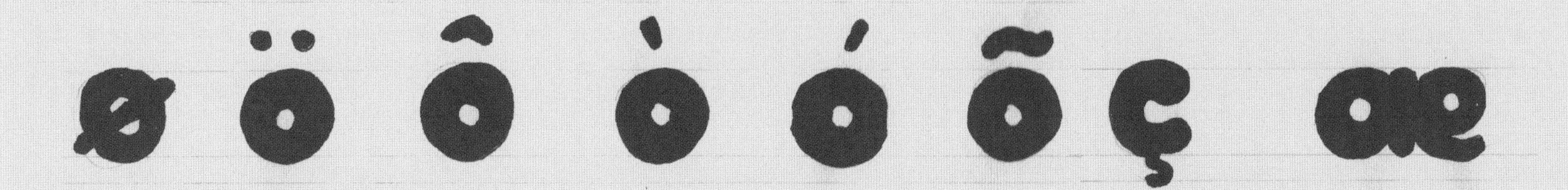

Numbers and special characters

1234567890

£€$&!?.,:;~’“”

Curly copperplate

This is my take on the traditional copperplate script, but with a flourish twist. It is a free-flowing style that is great for seasonal cards and invitations.

Pizza

Pizza

Curly copperplate alphabet

Aa Bb Cc Dd Ee

Ff Gg Hh Ii Jj

Kk Ll Mm Nn Oo

Pp Qq Rr Ss Tt Uu

Vv Ww Xx Yy Zz

Accents

å â à á ä é è ë ê

ø ö ô ò ó õ ç œ

Numbers and special characters

1 2 3 4 5 6 7 8 9 0

£ € $ & ! ? . , : ; ~ ' “ ”

Roman

This is a traditional font that has been around for centuries. It has always been widely used for engraving and etching, and is still commonly used today for honours boards and traditional British pubs. Take your time with this one, and really study the serifs and structure when practising.

Europe Europe

Roman alphabet

Aa Bb Cc Dd Ee

Ff Gg Hh Ii Jj

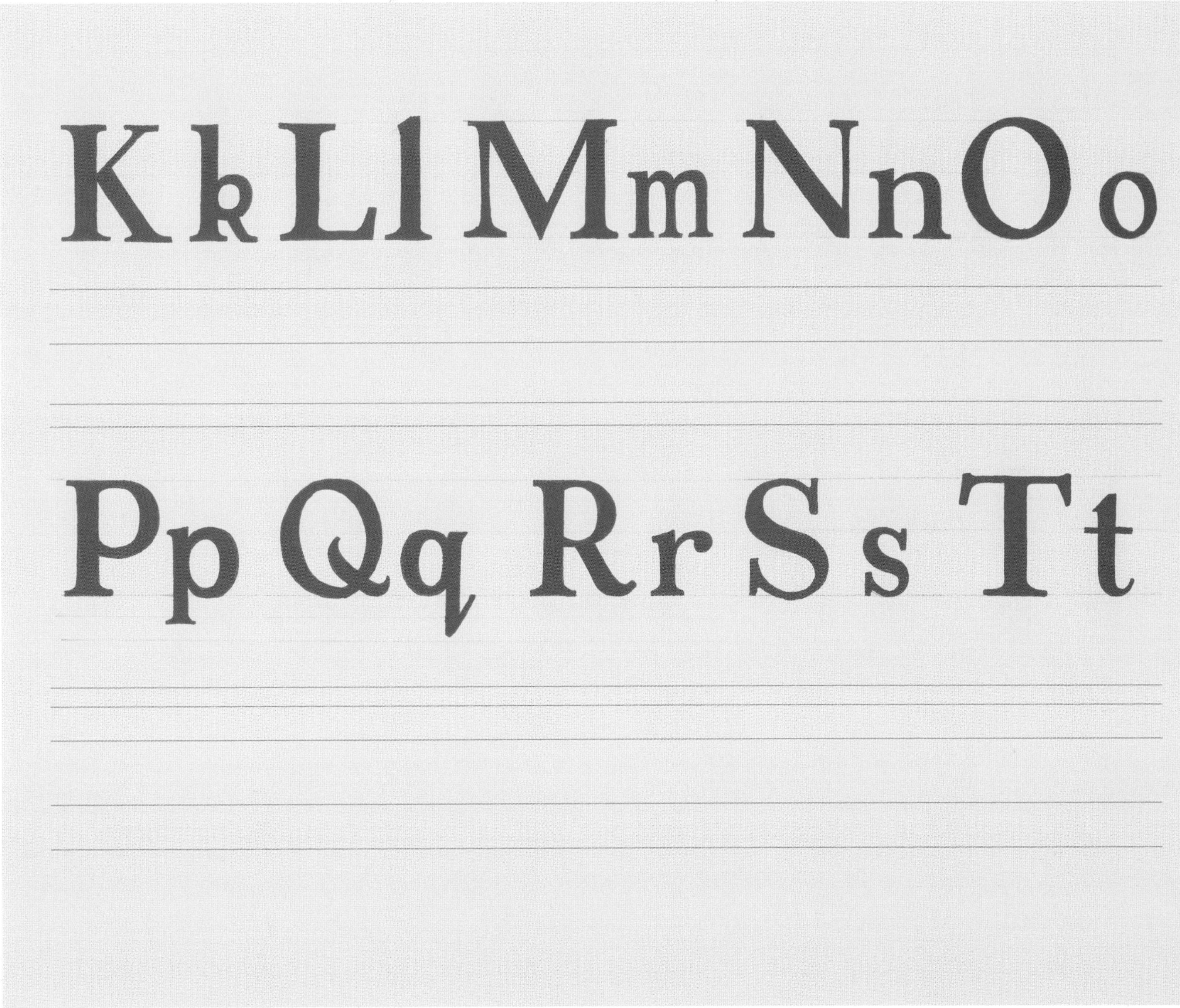

Kk Ll Mm Nn Oo

Pp Qq Rr Ss Tt

Uu Vv Ww Xx

Yy Zz

Accents

å â à á ä é è ë ê

ø ö ô ò ó õ ç æ

Numbers and special characters

1 2 3 4 5 6 7 8 9 0

£ € $ & ! ? . , : ; ~ ‚ ‘‘ ’’

Typewriter style

This is a really fun style to practise. It's best to keep the letters looking earthy and not perfectly straight, as you want them to look like they've been created by typewriter key strokes. It's a great style for a coffee shops and traditional cafés.

Menu Menu

Typewriter style alphabet

Aa Bb Cc Dd Ee

Ff Gg Hh Ii Jj

Kk Ll Mm Nn Oo

Pp Qq Rr Ss Tt

Uu Vv Ww Xx

Yy Zz

Accents

å â à á ä é è ë ê

ø ö ô ò ó õ ç æ

Numbers and special characters

1 2 3 4 5 6 7 8 9 0

£ € $ & ! ? . , : ; ~ ' " "

Funky block

I often use this for bars and personal projects—I think of it as my block with a bounce to it. When you paint the edges, make sure they are always uneven. Use narrow shapes when you curve the letters, and keep the style looking funky.

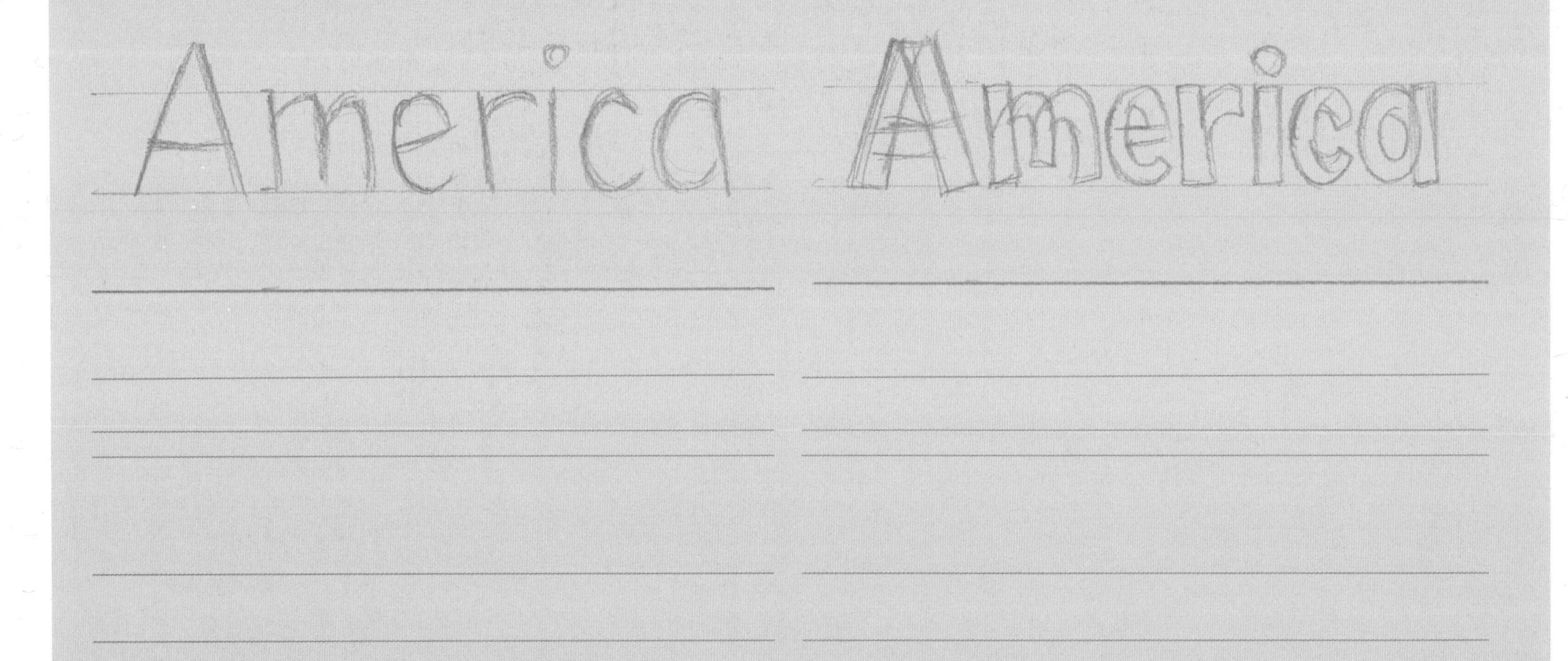

America

America

Funky block alphabet

Aa Bb Cc Dd Ee

Ff Gg Hh Ii Jj

Kk Ll Mm Nn Oo

Pp Qq Rr Ss Tt

Uu Vv Ww Xx Yy

Zz

Accents

å â à á ä é è ë

ê ø ö ô ò ó õ ç æ

Numbers and special characters

1 2 3 4 5 6 7 8 9 0

£ € $ & ! ? . , : ; ~ ' " "

Thin minimal

This is a refined minimalist block. Keep the lines as straight as you can, and be disciplined with the thickness of each stroke. Use block as reference, but make your strokes a lot thinner than you would for the block style.

Sport

Sport

Thin minimal alphabet

Aa Bb Cc Dd Ee

Ff Gg Hh Ii Jj Kk

Ll Mm Nn Oo Pp Qq

Rr Ss Tt Uu Vv

Ww Xx Yy Zz

Accents

å â à á ä é è ë ê

ø ö ô ò ó õ ç œ

Numbers and special characters

1 2 3 4 5 6 7 8 9 0

£ € $ & ! ? . , : ; ~ „ “ ”

Very slim casual

This letterform is inspired by the casual style, which is a popular signpainter's lettering style. Make sure the edges have nice curves to them, and try not to be too accurate when painting. This one is all about keeping a flow and a casual style.

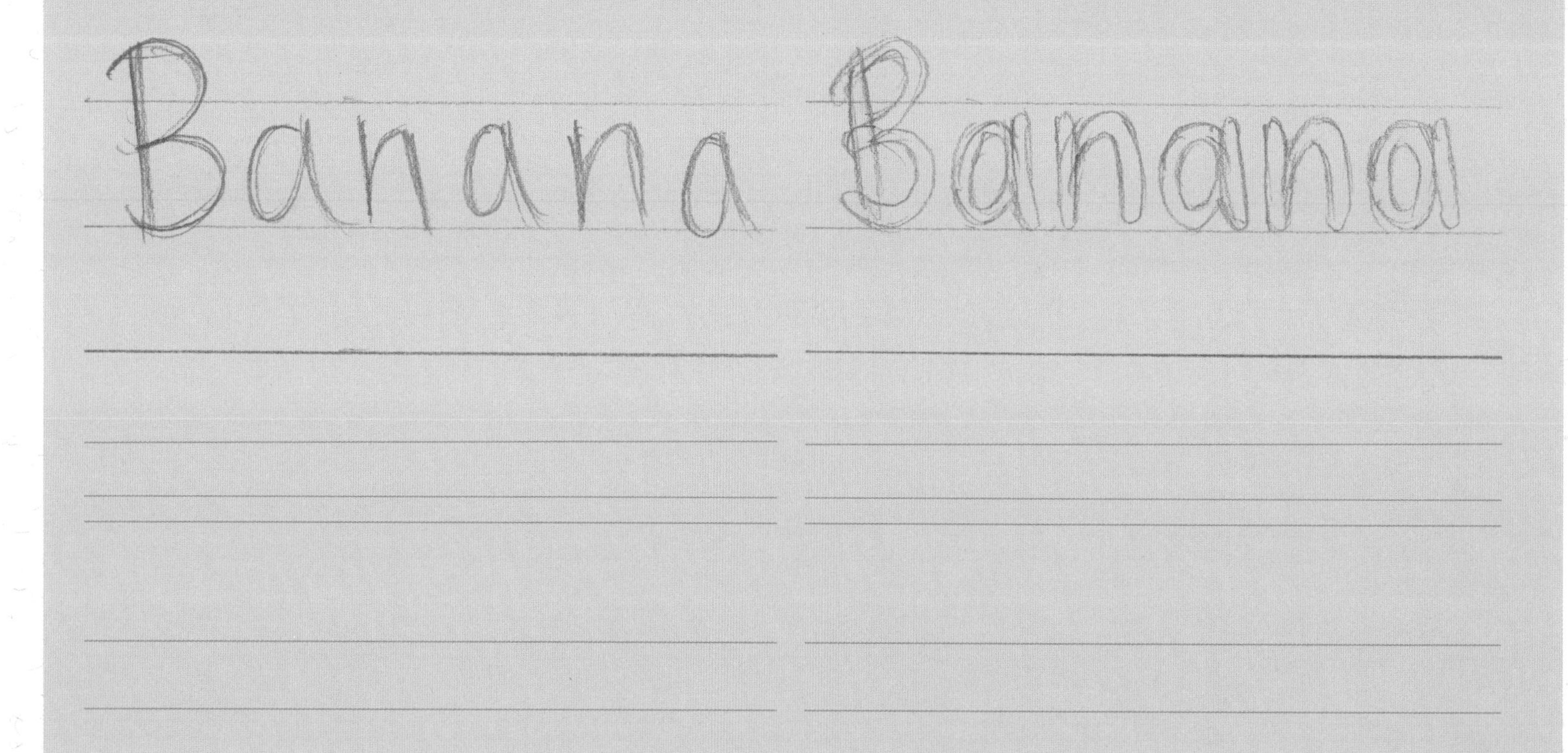

Banana Banana

Very slim casual alphabet

Aa Bb Cc Dd Ee

Ff Gg Hh Ii Jj

Kk Ll Mm Nn Oo

Pp Qq Rr Ss Tt

Uu Vv Ww Xx

Yy Zz

Accents

å â à á ä é è ë ê

ø ö ô ò ó õ ç œ

Numbers and special characters

1 2 3 4 5 6 7 8 9 0

£ € $ & ! ? . , : ; ~ ’ “ ”

Looking at artwork for inspiration

I have always been inspired by the typography used on vinyl album artwork covers, film posters and the many hand-lettering books that I have collected over the years. I use these platforms as inspiration for my work because they are things that I am interested in, and I always think it's good to analyse and study letters. Once you start doing this yourself, it will enable you to discover shapes and colour schemes that you may want to use and improve in your work. Be brave with your letters, and in time you will even be able to create your own letteform styles.

ABCDEFGHIJ
KLMNOPQRS
TUVWXYZ
abcdefghijklmno
pqrstuvwxyz
THE
CELL
PHONE
BOOTH
IS
OUT
Ride 'im
Fisherman!
RIO GRANDE VALLEY
FISHING
RODEO
PORT ISABEL, TEX.
AUG.
8-12
RESINOL
TAKES THE
FIRE
OUT OF BURNS
FOR SURFACE BURNS
I'LL
GIVE
YOU
$20.00
for
it
NOW I EAT
DOUGHNUTS
Upset Stomach Goes
in Jiffy with Bell-ans
BELL-ANS

Shadowing

Adding a shadow to a word is a great way to make it stand out from the crowd, and it's an extra step that can make a final piece look very striking and effective. You can either add your shadow to the left or the right of each letter, but always keep its position consistent throughout the piece.

- First of all, draw your grid lines and paint the first letter.
- I would then draw a small sun with a pencil, placing it somewhere on the top right or left corner of the letter. Here, it's on the top right.
- The position of the sun will help you to work out where the letter's shadow should go.
- Next, outline your shadow, and be realistic about how thick it would actually be.
- Once you have pencilled in your shadow, fill it in with black, then rub out the pencil marks. Or, if you are doing this on a blackboard, you can fill in the letter with white and then outline the shadow with a thin white pen, and don't fill it in.
- You could also use dark colours as a shadow on a blackboard.

Adding colour

When working on a blackboard, adding colour to a letter probably isn't something that you'll want to do too often. But if it's done subtly and with a colour that is bright enough to complement the white paint on the board, then you can create a nice effect. Try to use light, neutral colours.

- First, fill in your letters with white paint.
- Once filled in, add colour paint from the bottom of the letter going upwards.
- For a nice smooth effect, use the tip of your finger to carefully smudge the coloured paint from the top while it's still drying. This makes the coloured area blend nicely into the white, giving a subtle effect.

Which parts to highlight

The use of outlines and highlights on letters can be a really effective way of making the words and letters pop out. Even using a thin outline around the word or a thin letterform inside the letter with a bright colour can give your painted words an eye-catching effect. Use the examples here as something to work from when practising.

Borders

Adding a decorative border to your blackboard can be a really nice finishing touch to your piece. Even a simple line border can be really effective, and I like to use an ochre brown because it complements black and white very well. Floral decorations with wobbly border lines can look really nice too. When you do a border, however, always make sure you give yourself enough negative space around the letters so that the board doesn't look too cluttered.

CRAFTY
FELLAS
LONDON
CRAFT BEER
SPIRITS
WINE
CIDER

Cheerz

THE SHAKES
THE BIG BREKKIE: £6.50
ALMOND MILK, BANANA, OATS, CHIA SEEDS, ALMOND BUTTER, BLUEBERRIES, VANILLA PROTEIN
THE ALMOND FEATHERWEIGHT: £6.50
ALMOND MILK, BANANA, ALMOND BUTTER, DATES, MACA, VANILLA PROTEIN
THE SUCKERPUNCH: £6
COCONUT WATER, STRAWBERRY, BANANA, DATES, VANILLA PROTEIN
THE BLUEBERRY BRAWLER: £5
COCONUT WATER, BLUEBERRIES, VANILLA PROTEIN
THE PEANUT UPPERCUT: £5
ALMOND MILK, BANANA, PEANUT BUTTER, CHOCOLATE PROTEIN (SWAP FOR VANILLA PROTEIN)
THE LIGHTWEIGHT: £4
ALMOND MILK, VANILLA PROTEIN (SWAP FOR CHOCOLATE PROTEIN)
VEGAN PROTEIN AVAILABLE FOR ALL SHAKES
THE EXTRAS
EXTRA PROTEIN SCOOP £2
COCONUT MILK 50p
NUT BUTTER £1.50
COFFEE HIT 50p
MINT 50p
THE SHOTS
GINGER: £2.50
GINGER, LEMON
FIERY GINGER: £3
THE BLACKBOARD ARTIST

AUTHENTIC
WINGMANS
WINGERY

Cocktails
£6.80 each
Mojito

SPIRITS & MIXER
£2.50
COCKTAIL TEAPOTS
THE BLACKBOARD ARTIST

OPEN FOR:
WEEKEND BRUNCH
LUNCH
DINNER
SUNDAY ROAST
COCKTAILS & BAR SNACKS
A Drink with a view...